My Kingdom for a Horse

The story of a journey on horseback from the Cornish Moors to the Scottish Border

by

Margaret Leigh

The Long Riders' Guild Press

www.thelongridersguild.com

ISBN: 1-59048-029-5

To the Reader:

The editors and publishers of The Long Riders' Guild Press faced significant technical and financial difficulties in bringing this and the other titles in the Equestrian Travel Classics collection to the light of day.

Though the authors represented in this international series envisioned their stories being shared for generations to come, all too often that was not the case. Sadly, many of the books now being published by The Long Riders' Guild Press were discovered gracing the bookshelves of rare book dealers, adorned with princely prices that placed them out of financial reach of the common reader. The remainder were found lying neglected on the scrap heap of history, their once-proud stories forgotten, their once-glorious covers stained by the toil of time and a host of indifferent previous owners.

However The Long Riders' Guild Press passionately believes that this book, and its literary sisters, remain of global interest and importance. We stand committed, therefore, to bringing our readers the best copy of these classics at the most affordable price. The copy which you now hold may have small blemishes originating from the master text.

We apologize in advance for any defects of this nature.

Foreword

IN a stable in Scotland hangs an old Cornish bridle
with a tarnished brazen star on the brow-band.
This, if I can ever rouse myself to send it to town,
will bear the inscription BLISLAND TO RIDDINGS,
SEPT. 4–OCT. 5, 1938 : and Ladybird, the bay mare
who travelled the 560-odd miles between these points,
can wear it as a medal. For she is the heroine of
the piece, while the rest of our cavalcade are only
supers or at best showmen. When I hitched her to
the railings of that obscure station on the Border, I
thought to myself, " Well, that's that ; and I am not
sorry it's over ", while Ladybird, little suspecting
that this was the end, cropped the green grass beside
the line as if ready to pass the rest of her days on the
road, and to spend each night in a different field. It
sounds like heroism, but is really habit, the pleasant
belief that to-morrow will be just like to-day, which
makes well-handled animals contented and easy to
train. But I, being restless and human, was glad to
finish, to get on to something new. The name of
Riddings, which is no invention, but may be found
in the time-tables of the L.N.E.R., seemed richly

symbolical. Here, having scrapped all else, I could finally scrap the ride itself and become an ordinary person travelling by train. " This trek ", I thought, as I went in search of the station-master, " will be pleasant to look back upon." So it has proved, and not less pleasant, I think, in the actual doing. But the merit of all things temporal is that they come to an end, and most of us are like fidgety children who think " Amen " the finest word in the Prayer Book.

What follows is the record of a journey on horse-back from Bodmin Moor in Cornwall to Riddings, an obscure junction on the south bank of the river Liddel, which at this point divides England from Scotland. The distance covered was about 560 miles in 28 marching days, for we never travelled on Sunday, except in the last week, when stress of weather made me anxious to have done. For the first and longer part of the journey, from Newton to Hartington in Derbyshire, I had a companion and a pack-horse, and we camped each night in the field where the ponies grazed. Could we have started earlier in the year, we might have completed the trek in the same way ; but rapidly shortening days, and the slowness of the two older horses on hilly roads, forced us to reorganise. At Hartington we abandoned the pack-horse and camping equipment. My companion went home, while I pushed on alone with the best pony, trusting to luck for the night's lodging.

Foreword

I have often been asked if this trek was made for a wager. Hardly : for there is nothing adventurous, nor even very strenuous, in a horseback journey on English roads. In a country so thoroughly mapped, organised, and provisioned, fast traffic is the only danger, and all one needs is plodding patience, and the sense to keep off major roads and away from large towns. With quiet horses, good weather, and reasonably short daily marches, a ride of some weeks' duration is within anyone's compass, though the business of swimming against the stream is often a trial to nerves and temper. For riding is a slow, anachronistic mode of travel, and nothing is ready for the horseman, neither stabling, nor corn, nor a decent surface to ride on. He must find his own routes and make his own arrangements as he goes. Everything depends on the good-will of local farmers : but in my own experience there is a widespread interest in and sympathy with horses and horsemen. Only once were we refused a night's grazing, and this because the farmer was away and his wife afraid of strangers.

Still more often have I been asked why I was riding from Cornwall to Scotland when it would have been much quicker and easier to go by car or by train. The answer is quite simple. There is a Scottish students' song which begins : "*Shon Campbell went to college because he wanted to*". No need to go further. And yet, I might add that it would

3

be an experience interesting to myself and to any others who cared to read about it. I wanted to return to Scotland with my pony, and a horse-box is very expensive. I wanted to learn the technique of long-distance horseback travelling under easy conditions in a civilised country, and then see whether I had sufficient strength and resource to do the same thing in wilder places. I wished also to get a panoramic view of English farming from one end of the country to another, though so rapid and partial a survey could have no value except as a personal impression.

And the personal impression is a little sad. I have been through the length of my native land, and do not like it as much as I ought. That is, the England we have been busy making for the last thirty years. I am old enough to have memories of a quieter, more gracious age, and my younger readers must forgive me if I cannot view the mechanisation of our daily life with the proper enthusiasm. I lived for a dozen years among hills and empty moors, and then came blinking into the new day, and quite naturally did not feel at home. So that there may be something bat-like in the outlook of this book, which in an evil moment I was tempted to call " England no More ". For all this I ask your indulgence.

Never were there more cars on the road than in the present year, and yet, by the inevitable force of reaction, the number of saddle horses is ever on the increase. Dozens of people have said : " How much I envy you ! " Long-distance riding is not all fun, indeed it is often the reverse, but it is well worth trying for a season, and most certainly worth reading about in an armchair, or considering for one of those holidays when to-morrow is never spoilt by becoming to-day.

II

Preparations

THIS chapter should be skipped by the expert horseman and practical camper. Nor will it interest those who take no pleasure in the peculiarities of horses and the intriguing details of saddlery and camping equipment. It is written for amateurs by an amateur, mainly to indicate the pitfalls which the author has not had the sense or the luck to avoid. There was once a man who failed nine times for his degree, but was at last let through, perhaps because the examiners were tired of seeing the old familiar face. No sooner passed than he set up as a coach. " At any rate ", they said, " he has made all possible mistakes, and what he has not said must certainly be right."

Although the trek was planned in the spring of 1938, I could not hope to start before the first week in September. This was much too late, but there was no help for it, as my milk contract would not be completed till August 31, and after that must come the sale of stock and implements at Newton. However, in the intervals of seeing the farm through its last summer, I began to prepare for the road.

CONTENTS

		PAGE
I.	FOREWORD	1
II.	PREPARATIONS	6
III.	CORNWALL	20
IV.	DEVON	40
V.	SOMERSET	78
VI.	GLOUCESTERSHIRE	112
VII.	WARWICKSHIRE	142
VIII.	DERBYSHIRE	176
IX.	YORKSHIRE	210
X.	WESTMORELAND AND CUMBERLAND	244
EPILOGUE : IN A HORSEBOX		272

LADYBIRD, on the Derbyshire Hills, near Sterndale, nineteen days out from Bodmin Moor . . . . *Frontispiece*

Map of the Journey . . . *End papers*

Ladybird on the Derbyshire hills near Sterndale, 19 days out from Bodmin Moor

Preparations

Much of the work was useless ; but one learns by experience, and must reckon that of the stuff so carefully made ready, one quarter will be abandoned at the start, and half be thrown away upon the march. This is true even of important and well-organised expeditions : and when you have strewn your route with useless gadgets, and arrive with nothing but your saddle and waterproof, it is comforting to think that better men than you, with more valuable equipment, have done the same thing. The happy traveller, like the successful bridge player, must know what to discard : and the more he discards, the happier he will be.

Horses.—I had intended to take two of the three horses already at Newton, one for riding, and the other to carry the pack. Judy, the black mare, was too slow and heavy, with soft feet that would soon go to pieces on the hard roads. There remained Joey, a nine-year-old bay gelding just under thirteen hands, and Jenny, a bay mare about a hand higher, but several years older. Both these horses had been with me since my first days at Newton, and I knew them thoroughly. Both were sound, hardy, and believed quiet in traffic. Jenny had been working all winter and spring in chains, while Joey, an excellent stock pony, was used daily for herding sheep and cattle. I thought I had solved the problem of suitable mounts, but this was a bad mistake. In June a neighbour's stallion escaped to the moor, and Jenny climbed the boundary wall to join him. An autumn journey would do her no active harm ; but when in foal she tended to lose condition, and to be full of incalculable fancies, which made her uncertain in traffic. Then one morning in the middle of July we found Joey hobbling on three legs, with the fourth much swollen and inflamed about the fetlock. I sent for the vet, who said that he had injured the tendon sheath, and would not be fit to travel. Actually he was well in a month, and went with us as far as Glastonbury ; but he was the smallest of our ponies, and I doubt if he could have managed the whole journey.

I decided to take Jenny as pack-horse, and find another mount for myself. What I wanted was a strong solid cob of about fourteen hands, with clean feet and quiet on the roads ; but this was hard to procure. I could have had dozens of ponies and plenty of hunters ; but in Cornwall, a land of big hills and small farms, cobs are in great demand and rather scarce. I was offered a good-looking brown mare, fast and hard as nails, but she was too " hot " for my purpose, and being fresh from the moors had hardly ever seen a car. Then I tried a four-year-old gelding, who would pass anything on the road, but was rather quieter than a young horse should have been. Later he developed a strained shoulder, caused by over-pulling in a mower, and was rejected, not without sorrow, for he was an amiable beast. By this time there were only a few days left, and I had to take what I could get. Martha was a brown mare of uncertain age, with good withers, clean legs, and a well-carried head ; she had plenty of spirit, and was easy to catch and pleasant to ride. But we could not keep her fat, and though she did well at first, it was plain that she would never manage the hilly roads of the North. At Glastonbury she was exchanged for a bay gelding, of whom more in its proper place.

My travelling companion, Spencer, provided his own mount. At the last moment, after much running to and fro, he bought Ladybird, a charming bay mare, seven years old and just under fourteen hands. This pony proved the best of the lot, and the only one to complete the journey.

I have no technical knowledge of horses, but one learns much from experience, and I am sure that the best mount for a long journey is not a hunter or a riding-school hack, but a solid, hardy farm cob or herdsman's pony, with plenty of grit and endurance, easy to catch and quiet in traffic.

In long-distance riding the walk is the pace that counts, and a fast walker, with long smooth stride, is always to be preferred. The pack-horse should be narrow, smooth-paced, and at least as fast as the leader. For a led horse always tends to drag, and if he is also a slow walker, the whole troop will be delayed. In theory, all trek horses should be exercised beforehand, on gradually lengthening marches, with the saddles, riders, and loads they are expected to carry.   But there is rarely time for this, and if one chooses young and hardy ponies in regular work, there is little fear of a breakdown.   Some weeks before the start I wrote to a riding-paper for advice, which in the stress of work we were unable to follow : but I do not think the horses suffered.   We never exceeded twenty-five miles a day, and mostly did less.   We never travelled on Sunday, and as long as we had the pack, there was no trotting.   This kind of travel is, I am sure, less hard on horses than hunting three days a week, or regular ploughing. The chief difficulty is the hardness of the roads, but much may be done by keeping to the by-ways and grass verges, and if your horse has really sound feet, he will not suffer much.   As the old groom said, " It's not the 'ackin' nor the 'untin', nor yet the 'oppin' over 'edges as 'urts the 'osses' 'oofs, but the 'ammer, 'ammer, 'ammer on the 'ard 'igh road ". There is also a danger of sore backs and girth galls ; but if the saddles fit properly and are repadded before starting, and the horses are carefully watched for signs of incipient sores, the risk is not very great.   From first to last we had no trouble of this kind.   For summer or autumn travel no stabling is required. Every farmer has a sheltered field, and it is hardly ever refused.   Night and midday grazing will supply the bulky part of the horse's ration, and a few feeds of crushed oats can be carried on the pack-saddle or in front of the rider.

And after the horses, the horseman. " Don't you go," said my old landlord, with great earnestness. " You'll be stiff and sore for life. You won't listen now, but some day you'll remember what I said." He was too pessimistic. The first week out I was a little stiff and a little sore, but nothing to matter : and after that I got hard and could have continued indefinitely. Those who are used to riding need not worry, and much depends on having a suitable saddle. Personally, I found that a sheepskin pad on top of the saddle was a great comfort, preventing friction and soreness ; but my comrade jeered at such luxury, and doubtless a better rider would not have required it. I had the further disadvantage of starting tired ; and I am sure that a good horseman, fit and fresh at the start, would make light work of a ride of several weeks.

So much for physical fitness, which is perhaps less important than the right state of mind. The rush of modern life has made us impatient of delay, and most of us find it hard to adapt ourselves to the slow pace of travel on horseback. On English roads there are no thrills, no adventures, hardly any danger, but plenty of petty discomforts and unforeseen checks, which demand an unfailing supply of patience and good temper, with a robust cheerfulness and sense of humour. And if the traveller is to get any lasting pleasure and profit from his journey, he must be quick to observe the many beautiful and interesting things (most of them quite small) that lie along the road, waiting for the seeing eye to discern them.

Saddlery.—Spencer had a light hunting-saddle, on which nothing was carried but a waterproof strapped to the front dees, and when needed, a bag containing 14–20 lb. of crushed oats, with the weight hanging evenly on either side. I had an Indian cavalry saddle. It was rather heavy, but very comfortable and extremely well made. Military saddles have plenty of dees, and are useful when there is no pack-horse, and all equipment is carried by the rider. And now a word of warning about military saddles. You see a whole collection of handy-looking dees, and start tying things on with string, until the saddle looks like a stall at a jumble sale. Then having mounted with difficulty, you advance a certain distance, till thumping and rattling noises, increasing with every step, warn you that things are working loose. You proceed a bit further, and the thumping changes to intermittent dull thuds as one thing after another falls to the ground. Without trial, it is hard to realise how quickly the movement of a horse, even at a walk, will slacken the knots of string most firmly tied ; and even if the string holds, the package will be gradually disintegrated by the everlasting bumping on the saddle, or worse still, against the horse's warm moist flank. Blankets, coats, or bedding should be rolled firmly and fastened to the front or back dees with straps which can be tightened as required, while miscellaneous articles should be packed in stout canvas wallets which are fixed to the dees with straps or spring-hooks.

The wallets should be very strongly made, and preferably double on the inner side. Food, or anything perishable, should be packed in tins inside the wallets. It is a safe rule to have everything three times as durable as you think necessary. There is no doubt that for real comfort in riding, nothing whatever should be carried on the saddle, and the long-distance rider who travels *de luxe* will have his equipment sent on by car. But this is hardly playing the game.

For the sake of economy and independence I had decided to camp, and to carry our tents and bedding and personal belongings on a led pack-horse. After much enquiry I found a military pack-saddle as described in the *Army Manual of Horsemastership and Animal Transport*. This little book, which costs half a crown, proved most valuable, not only for the technique of loading and roping, but for its numerous hints on the management of horses on the march. The saddle was made in 1916, but it looked too fresh to have seen much active service. It consisted of two leather pannels stuffed with horsehair, and connected by iron arches back and front, which were hinged to fit any size of horse. The arches were fixed to wooden side-bars, which slipped into pockets on the pannels, and were fitted with baggage hooks, two on each side. The saddle had webbing girths, and was further secured by a leather breeching, crupper, and breast collar. It had, however, one serious defect. Instead of a single broad girth with a V attachment, there were two narrow girths, buckling high up, as on a riding saddle. This sounds a trivial thing, but it makes all the difference in practice. The broad girth with V attachment can be tightened without shifting the load, whereas the narrow girths have their buckles under the load, and cannot be adjusted without unpacking. The narrow-girth pattern is now obsolete, and well it may be. The wonder is that it was tolerated for so long.

The full army load is 150 lb., but this being dead weight, it is better to carry rather less. For our personal belongings, I got the saddler to make two valises of waterproof canvas, measuring 14″ × 16″ × 4″, with leather gussets, corners, and binding. The top back side was strengthened with webbing, to which were stitched two rings to fit the hooks on the side-bars of the saddle. These valises were excellent ; they never shifted or sagged, but if I could do things over again, I would make them a good deal larger and dispense with a top load, which for amateurs is nothing but a nuisance. In addition we had three heavy canvas kitbags fitted with loops through which the baggage rope could be threaded. They held our tents, bedding, utensils, and non-perishable stores. They were loaded above the valises, and secured by the free ends of the same rope. In wet weather the load was covered with one of the ground-sheets, and the whole secured by a surcingle of webbing with leather straps. This surcingle was not a success. All saddler's work is expensive, and wishing to save, I made it myself from a length of upholsterer's webbing, to which I stitched a strap and buckle from an old set of trap-harness. There was nothing wrong with leather or stitching, but the webbing was not strong enough, and in spite of the numerous holes we punched in the strap, the wretched thing was always too long or too short for the load proposed. And as the surcingle must on no account touch the horse's belly, we had to make an extra girth with loops to carry it.

The riding horses had ordinary snaffle bridles, and the pack-horse a cart bridle with blinkers and a long leading rein. All were supplied with leather night-halters, which for convenience in tying up at shops or houses, were worn all day beneath the bridles. We also made a picket-line, with rings at six-foot intervals, but this was scrapped before starting, and we never missed it. For grooming we carried a dandy-brush, curry-comb, and sponge, also a small outfit for cleaning and mending harness. We had intended to take spare sets of shoes and nails, but the weight was formidable, and they were not really necessary, as there are still plenty of black-smiths.

Camping Equipment.— We carried two light tents — Spencer's of the usual canvas bivouac type with two poles and wooden pegs, and mine of fine Egyptian cotton, with a single pole and aluminium skewers. I had also a fly-sheet, which is well worth the small additional weight, for in wet weather the inner lining is always dry and you can touch it or stack your kit against it without causing a leak. We each had a ground-sheet, a down sleeping-bag, and an army blanket. In addition I had an air-mattress, which for all the derision of Spartans, I consider the finest part of the equipment. It weighs very little, and ensures a soft dry bed under any conditions. For cooking we had a small primus, a saucepan, kettle, and frying-pan, with a couple of enamel mugs and pannikins. There were two collapsible buckets and a folding basin. We had also candles, matches, a teapot, a few non-perishable stores, maps, a book or two, cameras, and writing materials. Our personal kit included a change of clothes, spare boots, and extra pullovers.

This equipment is simple enough, but in practice it always seemed too much, and the labour of packing and unpacking, and still more of keeping the stuff in tolerable preservation, cannot be believed without trial. From morning to night, from the tying of the last knot to the loosing of the first, the pack is in constant motion, swaying and rolling as the horse walks forward, and pulling on breast-collar or breeching as he climbs or descends a hill. Everything you want to keep clean must be put in small bags inside the larger ones, and everything that can be spoiled by wet or bent out of shape by straining on ropes should be kept in strong tins, and all eatables be handled as if they were thin-shelled eggs on a crossing to Ireland. Needless to say we did not do all this, but we ought to have done it.

Clothing.— In the matter of clothing, we were unlucky in choosing a season when there is much variation of temperature. In a five-weeks journey we passed from nearly 80° F. in a heat wave in Somerset to 29° F. on a frosty morning in the Cotswolds, and from the steaming warmth of Devon to a howling gale on the fells of Cumberland. Everyone has his own ideas about clothes, but I found cotton breeches more practical than woollen. They are cool in hot weather, and can be easily dried — a great matter when one lives under canvas. On cold days they can be supplemented underneath, and in heavy rain can be covered with the light mackintosh trousers worn by motor cyclists. Most people like to ride in boots, and they certainly look much smarter. But for a long day's trek I would rather wear shoes and cycling stockings, especially when there are intervals on foot to save the horse.

Maps.— A good map is essential. To fix our general direction, we used a touring map of England, the scale being about eight miles to the inch. From this we calculated which sheets of the one-inch Ordnance Survey would be needed, and ordered them beforehand from the publishing office in Southampton. Never trust to getting maps by the way; these can be bought only in large town or tourist centres. The sheets should be of the canvas-mounted variety: the paper kind melt away in the rain. I was at great pains to make a transparent map-holder from the talc wind-screen of a derelict car, but lost it on the first day out; and this, like many another gadget, was never missed. The maps were expensive, for one sheet on an average lasted no more than two days. But the one-inch size is essential, for it alone shows the by-ways and un-metalled roads that suit the horseman. Above all, have faith in your map, and never darken counsel by asking the way. On several occasions we fell to the temptation and were misdirected. For the helpful native, accustomed to guiding motorists, will always send you to the main road, which you are studiously trying to avoid.

A word about expense. If you are willing to camp, your ride will cost you no more than a stay in country lodgings. The chief expenditure will be on horses and saddlery, for both must be good. The type of horse required can be bought for £15–£20 in most districts, and a good saddle for about £4–£5. Both horses and saddles can be sold again at the end of the trek ; but on the animals, which must usually be sold at once, one may lose something through being unable to wait for a market. The popularity of camping has made it easy to get all the usual camp equipment at moderate prices. As for your daily outgoings, the cost of food is what you choose to make it. The price of crushed oats for the horses is about a penny a pound, and they need 6–8 lb. a day. Our night's grazing at farms was often free, and at the most sixpence a head, with the camping-site included. Of course we were off the tourist track, and always explained to our hosts that we were not trippers, but farmers on tour, and this no doubt made a difference. But the countryman's interest in horses and riding is very real, and in most places we were received with open arms.

III

Cornwall

(1) *Preliminaries*

OUR first camp was made on the day of the sale
(Friday, September 2) in the little field behind the
barn at Newton. The entire contents of the house
were to be sold, and there would be nowhere else
to sleep. We had the sense to pitch the tents early,
knowing that by the time the sale was over and the
valuer's business completed, night would have fallen,
and ourselves not much inclined to grapple with
strange equipment in the dark. A farm sale is always
wearisome, especially when it is held at a distance
from the farm. There was no road to Newton, a
hindrance to buyers with cars ; so we borrowed
a neighbour's meadow which adjoined the cottage
where I had been living for the past year. The rain
had delayed the harvest, and the field was not mown
till late in August. But the hay was carried in time
for us to cart down the implements and other dead
stock, and arrange the various oddments in tempting
lots upon the ground. On the morning of the 2nd
we shifted the cattle. A new-born calf was put on

the cart, which already contained the cooler and other dairy utensils, and the whole load covered with a pig net.

Then came the worst job of all — gathering and penning the sheep. On the previous day a lorry had come to the field with forty hurdles, and the men thought we should need the whole parish to help us sort and pen our little flock. Such is the sinister reputation of hill sheep in the lowlands.

My old landlord, who was fond of sheep and had a good horse, went with me to the moor, where the flock (or most of it) could be seen on the skyline. We left the dogs shut up, for on such ticklish occasions no dog is better than a bad one. They asked us why we had not brought them in the day before. With most sheep this would have been a good idea. But not with ours. I have never known the Newton Cheviots stay for more than two consecutive hours in any one place. We rode round them and soon had them off the moor and into the yard, where they had often been gathered for marking and shearing. Here we were joined by two more helpers, and the fun began. There is no hedge in Cornwall that cannot be scaled by frightened mountain sheep, and our only hope was to keep the flock moving at top speed, with no time to break back or scatter sideways. We ran, we shouted, we cracked whips and flapped bags. The sheep poured down the hill like spilt milk, and turned into the lane which leads from

the bottom of Newton fields to Meatherin. This
lane, very narrow and inches deep in mud, was
bordered by high banks crowned with trees and bushes
which formed an almost impenetrable barrier. Sheep
are dainty walkers and hate soft going : and like
many humans, are scared of narrow places. When
the mud got deep the leaders stopped, and the rear-
guard, hounded by men and ponies, piled on top of
them. Once more we bawled, hooted, and flapped
our bags, but without result. " Shout louder ! " the
old man cried to me. " What's the use of you ?
You ain't half shouting ! " I did my best but my
voice had gone hoarse and husky.

The lane was filled with a solid jam of sheep. My
companion dismounted, and throwing me his reins,
pushed his way to the front, waving his stick and
yelling like a maniac. The leaders began to move,
and the whole flock plunged forward. The end of the
lane, which emerged on a road leading directly to
the field we were bound for, was now in sight, and we
had the sheep advancing steadily towards it. Some
thoughtful neighbour opened the gate, and stood back
to turn the flock up the road. And then right in the
gateway a dog appeared. The leading sheep wavered.
" Go and sit down, you —— ! " someone shouted.
But the dog did not sit down : he let out a few
barks, and the flock broke and surged back upon its
shepherds. Fortunately the narrow lane was choked
with men and ponies, and they did not get far.

Somebody collared the dog, and the Cheviots reached the field in safety. No dog is better than a bad dog : and the worst dog is he who heads a flock unbidden and then barks. My own dog has done it once, and if ever he does it again, will be mine no more.

It was now getting late. I left Spencer to help the auctioneer's man with the sorting and penning, while I rushed to the cottage and began to evacuate its contents. There was a green in front on which the furniture and utensils could be displayed to advantage and sold without overcrowding. One or two people came up for an early view, and perhaps regretted it, as I persuaded them to help me out with a few of the heavier things. In the midst of all this hauling and pushing, Spencer appeared from the field with the news that both rams were missing. These two, an Exmoor and a Cheviot, were inseparable friends, and in summer, when their harem were tediously intent on lambs, would graze apart in masculine seclusion. I cannot imagine how we missed them, but it was now too late for a search, and they were left to be sold at the local sheep fair, which was held at the end of September.

The sale was timed to begin at 2 P.M., and everything in the field was ready, but half the household stuff was still in the cottage. We bundled it out as it came, dumping it in the first place handy. The sheep were sold first, then the cattle, and as so often happens, the highest price was made by the poorest milker, a nice-looking young cow, and freshly calved. The implements sold very well. The rusty old horse-rake, which had been renovated with one coat of vivid green paint, made more than its original price, and much of the junk was keenly competed for. I had two galvanised tubular milking-stools — very modern, but hard to sit on and not very steady, for their legs had been bent out of shape when used as a stick by infuriated milkmaids. I thought they might fetch threepence each, but two men lost their heads about them, and they made twice their value new !

The weather was very fine, and some of the farmers had stayed at home to save the corn. But their wives were there, and came in crowds to the sale of household goods on the green. The auctioneer went slowly round the circle, followed by a nimble assistant, who bundled the smaller things into strangely assorted lots and waved them high above his head. A knife, two forks, a Woolworth jug, and a dud alarum-clock would be offered, bought, and carried into the front room of the cottage, where the auctioneer's clerk sat at an extemporised table recording sales and taking the money. If you are at all interested in human nature, go to an auction, and watch your canniest and most thrifty neighbours, goaded by competition, landing themselves with things they do not want at prices they would never dream of paying in cold blood. Sometimes they find a genuine bargain, but more often they get a clock that will not go or a stove that will not burn. I have never been lucky with lamps, and at that time had what must have been the largest collection of duds in the parish. They all sold well, though not one of them was worth a penny. Anything of real and solid value is less esteemed, and in proportion makes less money. By six o'clock the green was cleared, and two hours later I received my cheque and went down to the Rectory for supper.

The trek should have started next day, which was Saturday ; but Spencer reported that Martha had a slight attack of colic. He stayed with her till evening, when she appeared much better, but would obviously be unfit to travel so soon. It was just as well, as I had not finished packing, and had no desire for anything but food and sleep.

Next morning I tidied up the empty cottage, laid out the camp equipment for inspection, and with praiseworthy detachment sat at the door of my tent, watching my neighbours cart the corn, which had been valued standing, to the rick they were building in the mowhay. When Cornish farms change hands at Michaelmas, it is customary for the outgoing tenant to sow the corn for the incoming tenant to save. This was lucky, for the harvest of 1938 was very late, and even the hay, for which I was responsible, was not fit to carry till the third week in August. Martha had quite recovered, and the horses were looking their best, for Spencer had groomed them thoroughly each day and trimmed their manes and tails. In the afternoon we put the closed bridle on Jenny and fitted the pack-saddle. Then having filled the valises and kit-bags with sacks, waterproofs, and stones, we loaded them very quietly and carefully from behind. Jenny was fourteen years old, if not a little more, but she was full of fancies, especially when in foal. She hated to have things handed up or tied to the saddle, and would bolt at the sight of anything strange in the hand of her rider. However, the blinkers prevented her from seeing the curious load on her back, and Spencer led her up and down without incident until one of the kit-bags, tilting slightly forward, caught her eye, and she began to plunge violently. But she had not much scope, and the bag was pulled back out of her sight, and all was peace again.

I went about saying good-bye to various people and taking photographs. The farm, with its gates repaired, with all the junk cleared up and stock away, looked empty and rather sad. Night fell, and the tents were pale in the dusk ; and later, when candles were lighted inside them, they glowed like huge dim lanterns on the grass. The air was very clear, with a tang of autumn, and we saw the ridge of Hawkstor sharp against the stars. I blew up the air mattress, wriggled into my sleeping-bag, and lay still. The dog Thos came into my tent for a time, and then, being bored or cold, made trial of Spencer's. But he never cared for a nomad's life, and after a while he rose, yawned, and retired to the barn, which cannot have been very comfortable, for all the sacks were gone, and all the straw, and there was not even a cat to purr on the top of a wool-bag.

That night I did not sleep very much. The mattress and sleeping-bag were comfortable, not to say luxurious, but I was filled with that restless excitement and foreboding which makes a journey's eve its most appalling moment. We long for change, for adventure, and when it is near would like to call it off. What madness led us here, we ask ourselves ; could we not even now get out of it ?

For some years I had been tied to a small farm with its endless work and anxieties : now I was as free as air, with nothing but the trek horses, and the auctioneer's cheque in my pocket. I was rid of all the clogging household junk that makes so much labour and gives so little satisfaction. As I watched it sold and dispersed, I had a sense of relief and even of elation. This, I suppose, is all wrong : the good housewife should feel as if her own body were being dismembered and offered for sale. But there it is : I have never cared for sticks, and never shall. Those who love their inanimate possessions are to be envied, for " dead stock " can always be bought for money and preserved, with the help of a little grease or polish, *in statu quo* ; and being already dead, it cannot die on you, or lose its affection, for it never had any. Yes, it was good to be free, but I should miss the animals. The sheep had been sold in small lots, and the flock as a unit had ceased to exist. I thought of the cows, wondering in what strange byres they were now tied, and whether Judy found a stranger's grass as sweet as ours, and how many times the Corncrake's new owners had hunted him out of the dairy.

Next day was Sunday, September 4, and the misfortunes that pursued us would justify all the grimmest Sabbatarian scruples. After a hearty breakfast we rolled up the tents, and Spencer went off to catch, groom, and saddle the horses. There were four in all, for Joey had been sold to Penelope, the daughter of my friends in Glastonbury, and was to be delivered complete with saddle and bridle. Meanwhile I set to work upon the valises and kit-bags. Everything was stowed as neatly and tightly as possible ; but it soon became clear that a number of things must be left behind. I scrapped the picket-rope, spare horse-shoes, hammer, milk-can, and a number of dry stores, but, even so, we were forced to put the grooming and harness-mending equipment, the nose-bags, and canvas buckets into a separate sack : and this receptacle, which bore the legend " Finest White Fish Meal ", was the cause of much trouble, as will be seen in the sequel.

Jenny was loaded with great care. The two valises were hung on the baggage hooks and formed a neat and compact side load, while the three kit-bags were placed lengthwise on the upper part of the saddle, with their ends resting upon and overlapping the front and back arches. We tried to rope the load with the "diamond hitch" described in the *Army Manual*, but what we achieved was not quite the correct thing. The load seemed firm enough, and Jenny surprisingly quiet, but there was no room for the extra sack. This we decided to load on Joey, who could carry it as far as Glastonbury. After that we must re-pack and scrap a few more superfluities. So we took the cavalry saddle from Martha and put it on Joey, so that the sack could be roped to its numerous dees. He was also to carry the two small wallets which were fixed by spring-hooks to the side dees. One of these contained the primus in its tin and a bottle of paraffin : the other some food, including half a loaf of bread.

All this rearrangement took time, and although we had risen at 6.30, it was nearly noon before we left Newton. The start was very quiet, and was witnessed by only four people, but it was not so quiet as the finish, which, as far as I know, was seen by no one.

(2) *Sept. 4 — Blisland to Hendra*

We turned up the rough lane which leads from the yard to the moor, with Thos barking joyfully in front of the horses. Spencer was riding Ladybird and leading Jenny, while I was on Martha with Joey in tow. Our route lay across the moor in a north-easterly direction towards Altarnun, leaving Brown Willy and Rough Tor on the left. The weather at least was kind. It was one of those fresh westerly days that show the moor at its best. The distances were sharp and clear : the sky was alive with brilliant rolling clouds which left a trail of shadows chasing on the hills. We had not gone a hundred yards before Spencer saw that Jenny's load was shifting, and called a halt. The bags themselves were in place, but the whole saddle was canting over to the near side, and as the girths were still tight it took some strength to pull it straight. We advanced another half-mile, with myself in the rear to watch the load, which was rolling heavily like a rudderless ship in a rough sea. Then some trifle — a jolt or the shifting of some package, disturbed the balance, and the saddle began to list again, this time to the off side. Another halt and readjustment. Spencer, who was mainly responsible for the loading, began to look grim ; and well he might, for we were only half a mile out and had over 560 miles to go ! At this moment, with unstudied tactlessness, a neighbour rode up to ask if we had seen the missing rams. Needless to say we had not, and he no doubt returned with the news that the Great Trek had broken down almost before it had started.

Cornwall

We continued for another half-mile or perhaps less. Then with ghastly suddenness the saddle slipped right over until the topmost kit-bag was almost touching the ground. This upset Jenny, who began to prance and caper, but Spencer had her on a short rein, and after spending some time in soothing and encouragement, we secretly loosened the buckles and let the load and saddle slip gently to the ground. Then we turned off the other horses to graze — luckily for us they were easy to catch — and re-loaded Jenny from the beginning, pulling the girths as tight as could be done with safety. The place was empty of life and with no witnesses of our humiliation but a few Devon cows. We thought of hitching the horses to the stones of a prehistoric circle, but on closer inspection they proved too big, and each had a pit at its base which prevented the ponies from coming close. A few days before, this circle, called the Trippet Stones, was used to stage the Cornish Gorsedd, a neo-bardic ceremony in which a number of elderly gentlemen in sky-blue robes emerged from a private bus and made long speeches in Cornish and English, to the accompaniment of a Celtic harp and a not very tuneful trumpet. There was a large crowd of onlookers, and beyond them a ring of mild-eyed cows and inquisitive sheep, but the most interesting spectator was a man from an outlying farm who sat motionless on his pony while they sang the Cornish version of " Land of our Fathers ", wondering no doubt what it was all about. But now, thank God, the bards and trumpeters were gone, leaving the cows and sheep alone to see our shame.

We had taken nearly three hours to make two miles, and should be lucky to reach the further side of the moor that night. We moved slowly forward, stopping every half-mile to adjust the pack. The inconvenience of the double girth arrangement was now obvious, for a horse on grass loses bulk on the march, so that after a time the girths need tightening, and this could not be done without shifting the load. To save Martha, who had lost condition with the colic, I walked a good deal, leading a horse with either hand. In these days the moor is understocked, and at the end of summer the thick weathered mat-grass, which in some places grows almost to the knee, makes very heavy going. The valley bottoms are flat and marshy, with bogs and "pisky beds" along the sluggish rivers, whose channels, deeply cut into the peat, are choked with rushes and oozy sphagnum moss, making them hard to ford except at places kept clear for the hunt. I had always been too busy on the farm to explore the more distant parts of the moor, and in the confusion at the Trippet Stones our map was left behind. So we wasted some time in prospecting for places to cross the various streams that rise in the marshes beneath Brown Willy. I had once got a horse belly-deep in a bog at the foot of this Tor, and was not anxious to repeat the experience.

Later, when we had forded one of these streams and were climbing the slope above it, came the worst moment of the whole trek. We were so much concerned with Jenny's big load that Joey's smaller one, consisting of nothing but a sack weighing perhaps 12 lb., and a couple of small 12″ × 8″ wallets, had received but little attention. A horseman appeared on the skyline, and wishing to make enquiries about the next ford, I touched up Martha and, with Joey in tow, trotted towards him. The cavalry saddle which Joey now carried was rather too big for him, and the girths too long ; and the sudden forward movement must have upset the balance of the load. There was a violent jerk which nearly unseated me, and the leading-rein was wrenched from my grasp. I turned to see Joey in full gallop with the saddle and load capsized beneath his belly. At every step his hind feet caught in the fans of the saddle, and the contact spurred him to wilder flight. Round and round he raced in big circles, gradually disembowelling the saddle. The air was thick with little bits of flocking, which floated on the breeze like thistledown. Now and again some object, ejected from wallets or sack, would fly through the air, until the whole load was strewn in a wide ring on the ground. But Joey was soft and fat from idleness, and being thoroughly blown, came to a halt beside the other horses, eyeing me with his usual philosophic detachment as if to say, " Well, that's that.

And now what are you going to do about it ? "

We began to inspect the damage. The leather of the saddle was intact, and the forward part of the padding still in place. But the lining behind was in ribbons, and every scrap of flocking gone on the wind. The saddle was repaired for the time being with string, and we went round the circle collecting the debris. One of the wallets was torn beyond repair, and the primus tin all battered and bent. The bottle of paraffin was unbroken, but there was no trace of provisions. A strange black dog, who had appeared with the indecent promptness of a vulture, was seen disappearing with something white in his mouth, no doubt the bread. This was a pity, for we were now rather hungry. Thos, who had done nothing to stop the thief, sat down and yawned. No one, he thought, could expect him to attack an adversary so much larger than himself. No one did. He is an amiable dog, but courage is not his strong suit. Then I noticed that Joey's forefoot was entangled in his rein, and as I stooped to lift it, he somehow caught me a rap on the nose with his knee, causing a whirl of stars and profuse bleeding, which delayed us for another twenty minutes.

The shadows were lengthening, and we hurried on as fast as the pack would allow us. We crossed the second river at a farm ford, and got directions from the farmer, who was much interested in our cavalcade, but a little incredulous when he heard we

were making for the Border. To the stay-at-home
Cornishman, Scotland is a remote and fabulous
country of ice and snow : and at that moment I felt
like sharing his scepticism. If to-day's march were
a fair average, we should be a year on the road.

Leaving the yard, we turned up a short enclosed
lane, where Jenny's load was once again removed and
unpacked. While Spencer was busy with the ropes
I took a photograph of this, our most characteristic
activity. At this point I must pay a tribute to Jenny.
She must have been sadly tried by the constant swaying and slipping of her unaccustomed load, and yet,
after the first caper at the Trippet Stones, she remained perfectly quiet and tractable. Had it been
otherwise, there would have been little hope for the
baggage. As for the other horses, Joey, having done
his damnedest, gave us no further trouble ; Martha,
as always, was exemplary ; while Ladybird did nothing worse than attempt to roll in her saddle.

Another mile or so brought us to Codda, a moorland " township " consisting of a couple of farm-
houses and a cottage or two on the banks of a stream.
The sun was setting. We had been travelling for
eight hours, and we debated whether we should camp
where we were, or push on to Altarnun. The
distance was about four and a half miles. This at
our present rate of progress would mean two or
three hours of experimental travelling in twilight and
then in darkness. But there would be a moon later,

and we decided to go on. I should have liked to camp at Codda, if only for the charm of its loneliness ; for it had that pensive and withdrawn beauty of all wild places at dusk, whether in Cornwall or Brittany, in Wales or Ireland or the Western Highlands of Scotland. The glen was no more than a shallow cup in the moor, full of bracken and gorse and the glimmer of granite boulders ; and beside the stream were enclosures of grass, cropped close by rabbits, which shone in the faint light with a vivid green that was almost fiery. There was no sound but the murmur of wind and water and the low of homing cattle.

We crossed a narrow bridge and turned up the hill, following a track on which abrupt slopes of loose stones were succeeded by level stretches of moss and marsh. The horses' feet rang sharply on the rock or squelched in sticky mud. At one point the path ended in a wide sheet of water, fringed with rushes and slime. Ladybird and Jenny crossed without hesitation, but Martha disliked wet feet, and no blows or exhortations of mine would induce her to move. At last she was driven over by Spencer, and we emerged upon a wide featureless plateau about 900 feet above the sea. There was still some light in the sky, enough to show a multiplicity of cart-tracks, perhaps centuries old, all leading in the same direction. These we followed in open order, each on a separate and parallel track, with the afterglow on our left cheeks. Faint stars appeared in the zenith, and above the long serrations of Brown Willy a planet hung, bright and sharp as a diamond. The air was keen and cold. We rode n silence, each alone with his thoughts. This tranquil movement through an empty world rocked me into a kind of trance, like that induced by sitting too long beside running water or moving tides. We might have been at any place on earth, and at any time in history, since horses were tamed and ridden. We were less ourselves than impersonal travellers under the open sky, looking for a place to pitch our tents and prepare our food.

Presently we saw points and clusters of light, far away, but unmistakably lamps, not stars ; and we knew that the nearer horizon of the moor had given place to a distant view of the " inland ", the culti- vated country that lies between Camelford and the shores of the Atlantic. Soon the tracks would descend right-handed and we should be at Altarnun. The level surface of the plateau had made easy going for Jenny, and we covered the last two miles with- out a halt. I love the moor, but the sight of those faint human lights gave me a thrill of pleasure, for soon we should find a place to camp, with rest and food.

At 9.30 we reached Hendra, an outlying farm in the parish of Altarnun. We knocked at the back door and explained our business to a sympathetic audience. The farmer offered us a field which, though full of poultry-houses, appeared to have some

grass. The moon had risen, and by its light we unloaded the pack and pitched the tents. The first
day's march was over. We had certainly crossed the
moor, but it had taken us ten hours to travel six
miles, and unless we could solve the problem of the
pack-saddle, we must either abandon the trek or
reorganise our transport.

We had pitched our tents hastily and in the dark,
troubling only to make them turn their backs to the
keen northerly breeze. Under the ground-sheets of
both tents were mysterious lumps and bulges, which
in the light of day were seen to be the cinders and
clinkers of an ash-heap levelled and scattered by hens
— a dry stance, but not very soft ! For a time the
candles burned, while Spencer, who had a personal
knowledge of East Cornwall and West Devon, marked
on the next sheet of the map our route for the coming
day. When you are travelling by minor roads and
unmetalled cart-tracks, it pays to mark the proposed
route in ink or heavy pencil, thus saving the trouble
of poring over a flapping sheet when mounted,
perhaps in wind or rain : for the roads that catch
your eye on the map are very rarely the ones you want
to follow. While he was thus occupied I wrote up
my diary, a curt affair in pencil, and not always very
legible, for in Cumberland the rain got into the rucksack in which it was carried.

I blew out the candle. The tent was full of
diffused moonlight, showing a pile of kit-bags and

saddles in the corner. I began to think hard, trying to discover what was wrong with the pack : was it the load, the roping, the saddle, or the horse ? Not the load, for it was compact, well-balanced, and yielding enough for the cords to bite into it. The roping, though unprofessional enough to make an A.S.C. sergeant-major explode with fury, was sufficient for a simple load on easy gradients ; and the saddle, apart from the vexatious double girths, was above criticism. I began to think that Jenny was far from being the ideal pack-horse, and further experience proved that her wide ribs and rolling gait were the chief cause of our trouble. After some consideration I decided to make a day's trial of riding her, with Martha as pack-horse.

The night wore on. Thos for a time lay curled beside me. Then he wormed his way under the closed flap and went to Spencer. Unlike most dogs he definitely preferred men. The horses roamed about the field, grazing in this place and that. Now and again I heard a shrill squeal as Martha, who had a shrewish temper, attacked the younger and more beautiful Ladybird. The mares had no male admirer but the plump and philosophic Joey, to whom, being mere companions, they were all equally attractive. But this did not prevent them from indulging in private feuds in the seclusion of the field, where they would sometimes gallop, cleverly avoiding the guy-ropes of the tent.

IV

Devon

(1) *Monday, Sept. 5 — Hendra*
to Lower Cookworthy

NEXT morning we rose at sunrise. The weather was still dry, with a cool north-westerly breeze. The primus, which was of the baby kind recommended to campers, had always been troublesome to light, and the battering received on the moor had not improved its condition. The little can of methylated spirit was almost empty and I cooked our breakfast over a fire of sticks, which crackled merrily enough until the kettle began to sing, and then without reason or warning expired in clouds of blinding smoke. I tried using the pump of the air-mattress as a bellows, but it was not a success, and the meal was cooked only by means of prolonged and personal blowing, while the sulky flame was fed with selected twigs, one at a time and broken very small. It took us three hours to cook and eat breakfast, strike camp, saddle the horses, and rope the load ; and even with practice we rarely finished more quickly. It sounds incredible, but trial will show that in this kind of travel you will spend nearly as much time and effort on camp work and packing as on the march itself. No wonder that travellers in outlandish places take hosts of native porters to carry their baggage, and servants to pitch their tents and prepare their food, so that they can devote all their attention to the actual planning and marching, and to the scientific observation, sport, or sheer enjoyment for which they have come. In our kind of travel you have roads and maps and farms and a good climate ; but you have also to do all your own animal management, packing, camping, porterage, cooking, photography, writing, and surveying, as well as the mere physical activity of getting from one point to another. It is all great fun, but it takes time and effort, and the first few days will always be a trying period of experiment, delay, fatigue, and minor annoyance, in which a lively sense of humour is more valuable than the most foolproof equipment.

Our second day's march was quite a success, and we started the routine that was followed throughout the trek. At 9.15, or at latest 9.30, we took the road and marched till about 1.30, with two short spells of ten minutes each, when the horses with slackened girths were allowed to graze on the roadside. At 1.30, or as soon after as we could find a suitable place to halt, we off-saddled for an hour and a half, and removed the pack. The odd half-hour was spent in loading and unloading. Some time during the morning I would stop at a village shop and buy the day's provisions. In the afternoon we marched from about 3 to 6.30, with two more spells of rest. By 6.30 or thereabouts we reckoned to have done our daily twenty miles, and began to look for a suitable farm at which we could find a night's grazing. It is an advantage to get a well-fenced field with shelter from the prevailing winds, where the horses can be turned loose to graze and roll as they please. Water is an advantage, but if there is none, they can drink at a trough when they arrive, and again before leaving in the morning. Picketing is troublesome, and in unskilled hands may be dangerous. If the horses are tied in a stable, they will need hay as well as corn ; and a horse accustomed to grass will often refuse hay in summer or early autumn.

We left Hendra at 9.30. I was in front on Jenny, with Joey in tow ; close behind came Spencer on Ladybird with Martha as pack-horse. Jenny was wide and tiring to ride, and the saddle did not suit me ; but Joey, who was devoted to the mare and kept as close to her as possible, was an ideal horse to lead. This time we divided the pack, letting Joey carry the two valises, and Martha the kit-bags. The pack-saddle fitted Martha to perfection ; she had narrow flanks and a smooth sedate walk, and I noticed that the load, instead of swaying in a wide arc, was oscillating gently, with no disturbance of vital balance. She was inclined to snap at Ladybird, but nothing to matter, and as long as Jenny was leading, kept up a fair and steady pace.

From the farm lane we emerged upon the main road to Exeter, which we followed as far as Five Lanes. There was a constant stream of traffic— lorries, and motor cycles and touring cars, mostly going east, whose occupants stared at us with interest and amusement. The surface was not very slippery, and the horses were quiet ; luckily for our first spell on a major road, we met no oil-tanks, livestock lorries, motor caravans, or pantechnicons. At Five Lanes, wishing to avoid the centre of Launceston, we turned left and pursued a minor road through Trewen, by which we could cross the river Kensey on the outskirts of the town. This road, which followed the valley and for most of its course kept in sight of the Southern Railway, was empty of traffic, and in contrast with yesterday's march, led us through rich dairy land, mostly in grass, with many trees and streams of running water. It struck me then, for the first but by no means the last time, that the English countryside, as we see it on a long and leisurely tour, has more variety in itself, and changes far more rapidly, than we are inclined to suppose. Except in parts of Warwickshire and Gloucestershire, each day's journey was quite different from those that preceded and followed it ; and on one occasion we passed in a single march from the typical Midland scenery of South Derbyshire to the bare limestone hills round Hartington.

The sky was partly overcast, with the type of cloud that suits the camera — sharp in colour and very definite in form. The visibility too was unusually good, and from every ridge we saw ahead of us the Dartmoor range, massive and purplish-black against the changing sky. Behind us, and a good deal lower, were the Cornish hills. In actual measured height Rough Tor and Brown Willy are not impressive. Both are less than 1400 feet, and rise not more than 500 feet above the general level of Bodmin Moor. But their craggy fantastic outline gives them a mountainous look which is more imposing than mere altitude. I was sorry to lose the sight of these hills, for now there was no more wild country between us and the High Peak of Derbyshire.

We met nothing but one or two local cars and a few old people out for a stroll, who gazed at us with great interest. Soon after one o'clock we reached a bosky lane near Tredundle, which dropped steeply to a stream flowing across the track. We crossed and watered the horses ; and on the further side found a secluded field, in which we off-saddled and had lunch. The horses were tied in a row along the hedge, and their saddles and loads removed. Then we turned them loose and spread our provisions. A score of Devon yearlings were grazing not far off, and after a while, urged by the

fearless curiosity of young cattle, they came closer and
began to sniff at the pile of kit. Time after time we
drove them away, but they always came back. In
the Launceston district and in West Devon, where
Spencer was personally known, we did not always
ask leave to enter a field for lunch ; had anyone
appeared, we should have explained our business and
offered to pay. Further east, we always asked permission first, and it was never refused. Nor was
the payment we offered ever accepted.

As we approached Launceston the level of the
road dropped, and we skirted the town near the
banks of the river. Turning left towards the bridge,
we came to a large flour-mill which had the greater
part of one wall laid open to the street. From this
yawning cavity, which revealed great piles of sacks
with half-seen shapes of workmen flitting among
them, came the strident clang of machinery. Jenny
stopped, threw up her head, and turned to bolt. I
pulled her round to face the peril, but no amount of
encouragement and heel-digging would make her
advance a step. Meantime Martha and Ladybird had
overtaken us, and urged by Spencer's superior horsemanship, were soon beyond the mill. Hoping to
follow this lead, I renewed my efforts, but Joey
merely looked blank and mulish, while Jenny began
to curvet sideways and backwards. The road, which
sloped steeply to the bridge, was polished and full of
traffic. I dismounted and tried to lead the horses

forwards. But Jenny planted her legs firmly apart and refused to budge. On the far side Spencer was patiently waiting with the others, and I was feeling vexed and humiliated, like one who in some public place chases his hat, or, hoarse and sweating, is flouted by a disobedient dog. Then a man jumped out of the mill and took Joey's bridle, and between us we coaxed the horses across. The British workman is the most helpful creature on earth, and I was duly grateful. Further on we met a baker's van and I bought a loaf of bread, which, owing to the destruction of the wallets, I was obliged to tie to the front dees. Near Lifton Down it fell off, thus showing the soundness of the advice offered in Chapter II. Luckily there was no dog about, and we ate it with relish for breakfast next morning.

At 5 P.M. we crossed the Tamar at Polson. This was an event, and I squandered sixpence on a telegram. There were many other rivers to cross before we reached the Border, but at least we had entered a new county on the second day out from Blisland. We were now back on A30, the main road to Exeter. There was a roar of traffic, but we proceeded without incident until we met an eight-wheeled lorry with a clashing load of long planks. Jenny, incalculable as ever, paid not the slightest attention, but Joey shied, causing his saddle to slip. I heard a thud, and turning, saw one of the valises lying on the ground. By this time he had come to regard saddle-slipping as a natural phenomenon, like rain or a cold wind, and merely looked stupid. The driver pulled up and, rescuing the valise, handed it to me. We drew into a gateway and re-packed Joey's load. After this incident we had no further trouble with it.

Before long we left the main road and turned north towards Lifton Down. We were on a high ridge, with wide views over the Tamar valley. The dark mass of Dartmoor was still before us, but looked much nearer, and its details were sharply defined, for the air was amazingly clear. The Cornish hills were far in the rear, and after that night we lost them altogether.

Spencer had an intimate knowledge of this country, and I was content to follow his lead. Towards sunset we reached Lower Cookworthy, a fair-sized farm in a sheltered and secluded valley. We decided to halt for the night, and Spencer went in to ask for grazing. The farmer was away at a sale, but we were well received by his wife, who showed us a field of good grass with water at the bottom. Here we unsaddled and pitched our tents. To a tired and hungry traveller, who at the end of a long march has to unpack and prepare his tent and bedding, there is nothing more wearisome than the cooking of supper, and I had made a private resolution that whenever possible we would persuade the farmers' wives to give us tea, with as much to eat with it as could in decency be asked for. At Cookworthy we made our request with some diffidence, for the house was very elegant and the lady of a rather intimidating refinement ; but she did not refuse, and we sat down to a glorious meal of tea, cold meat, pasties, tarts, and home-made cakes. Later the farmer came in with his son, and it was not very long before he and Spencer found a host of common acquaintances. My companion, who had been working on a Dartmoor farm and was mad about horses and hounds, had a wealth of farming and hunting talk, which entertained our agricultural hosts, and, we hoped, distinguished us from the ordinary hiker or tourist.

Later, replete and very sleepy, we retired to our tents. The saddles had been stored in a linhay, and we had plenty of room to work at maps and diaries. But we were tired, and candles were soon extinguished. I was just dropping off to sleep when I heard a sound of hoofs on the road. Someone riding home, I thought, and made no more of it. Some time later I was roused by a voice at Spencer's tent, and a few moments later he and the unknown man went off together. No one had called me, so I left them to it, and went to sleep. Next morning I heard that our visitor was employed on a night-shift at the Ambrosia Dairy in Lifton, and when cycling home had met a pony straying on the road. Somehow, by the telegraphic swiftness of country gossip, he had learnt that there were horsemen encamped at Cookworthy, and had come to warn us. The pony was Ladybird, who must have been rubbing her neck against the gate — a favourite trick of hers — and so loosened the catch. Had it been Jenny, the whole troop would have followed her back to Newton, for she was the recognised leader. We should then have been in a sorry plight. But in crossing the Tamar our luck had turned. It was not Jenny, but the mild and unenterprising Ladybird ; and this was the only time a horse broke out of the field at night. In every way the second day's march had been better than the first, and we logged nineteen miles.

(2) *Tuesday, Sept. 6 — Lower Cookworthy to West Risdon*

The night had been fine and cold, but before morning the wind shifted to the south, and we woke to a world obscured in drizzle and mist. We had to breakfast inside the tents, and packing was a dismal and protracted affair. My ground-sheet, made of heavy green Willesden canvas, was used to cover the pack. We were late in starting — it was 10 A.M. before we left the field, and the muggy warmth made it unpleasant to ride in heavy waterproofs. On such a day you must either wear your raincoat all the time and get hot, or not wear it at all and get wet, or keep taking it on and off, which, when you are riding with a led horse, usually means dismounting every half-mile. After a while the drizzle turned to drenching showers, with bright intervals between. Our route ran towards Inwardleigh by Bratton Clovelly, following a long ridge which stretches for many miles through Mid-Devon, parallel with Dartmoor. We were well abreast of the highest tors, and in clear weather the views would have been superb ; but the moor was hidden by drifting sheets of rain, and we saw no more than intermittent gleams of light on drenched and inky summits.

The road was a minor one and quiet : indeed we travelled all that day without touching a main thoroughfare. Some three miles out beyond Rexon I missed my camera, which must have been left behind at one of our numerous halts for shifting raincoats. While Spencer trotted back for it, I stayed with the other three ponies, letting them graze in a gateway. Although we had been only two days on the road, Newton seemed infinitely remote both in time and space. The trek, with all its contingencies pleasant and otherwise, stretched forward and backward indefinitely. We were as yet only thirty miles out, with a long journey ahead, and in choosing minor roads we were deliberately making it longer. We succeeded in crossing the Border without passing through any town larger than Warwick or Glossop, and without travelling more than an average of two or three miles a day on a major road. Had we had a detailed personal knowledge of the whole country traversed, we could have done much better. But the continual following of devious by-ways that merely link up farms or obscure villages, involves much loss of time, and if you are in a hurry to get somewhere, is not to be recommended. But no one who wishes to enjoy a riding-tour can afford to be in a hurry. Main-road travelling is hell for man and horse, and must at all costs be avoided.

Many people have asked me how in these days we could manage to dodge traffic. The answer is simple. Keep off all A roads, and as far as possible off the better variety of B road. Most ordinary motor traffic, and all heavy transport, is concentrated on the main thoroughfares, so that on a by-road, such as the Foss way in Warwickshire, you can ride for miles without meeting anything but an occasional farm cart, a labourer on his cycle, or the local doctor in his car. The motoring public sticks firmly to the major roads, and hardly knows of the existence of other and less-frequented tracks. You can avoid traffic almost anywhere in England, if you know where to go and are not in a hurry. The only exception is in mountainous districts where there may be only one pass, and consequently only one road.

In the west of England the harvest had been late and broken ; but we noticed that on the best and earliest land the corn was already carried. Higher up, however, most of it was still in the stook or even uncut, and in exposed fields the standing oats had been damaged by heavy wind and rain. The cattle were all North Devons, while the sheep were mostly Devon Close-wools, a newish breed evolved by skilful crossing. Many of these were folded on clover. The land, as everywhere in Devon, showed great variations of quality, from the deep rich loam of the valleys and lower slopes to sour and rushy uplands, which at this point would often break into heathy uncultivated down.

We were now in a purely agricultural district unknown to tourists, who rush in crowds to the moors and coast. Mid-Devon, like many another neglected district, has a quiet and individual charm. Just before noon we reached Bratton Clovelly, a large and pleasant village with a corn merchant's store and excellent shop. Here I bought cooked ham and tomatoes, bananas and chocolate and butter, while Spencer obtained a good supply of crushed oats for the horses. We posted a few cards, and then went on for a mile or so, till the sight of a small green meadow beside the road reminded us that it was past lunch-time. In one corner was a rick of hay to which they were carting rushes for thatching. We asked the men for leave to turn in. No sooner had we unsaddled than a heavy shower came down : the bags and saddles were hastily piled and covered, and we ate our food in the shelter of the hedge.

The rain did not last long, and the rest of the day was bright and clear. Crossing the railway near

Boasley, we followed a straight and grassy track which led towards Ashbury. On the further side of the line was an open stretch of rough pasture known as Venn Down, from which we could see far across the chequered undulations of the midland parishes, beyond which, like a grey cloudbank, lay the distant hills of Exmoor. South of Ashbury we turned right, and passed through a mile or two of heavily timbered country, where every farm-house and cottage had beside it an enormous pile of wood. Many of the trees were conifers ; and the empty road, with its iron railings and carpet of pine needles, looked like an avenue in a large and carefully planted park. This part of Devon, like all districts of small farms and frequent hamlets, is covered with a network of lanes, and at every few hundred yards we came to cross-roads with signposts. All the right turns appeared to lead to Okehampton, and all the left ones to Hatherleigh ; and later, when these two persistent names were replaced by others, we had a sense of relief and achievement. Our plan of avoiding built-up areas was constantly leading us *between* important places, and as the names of towns began to appear on signposts within a radius of about ten miles from their centres, we would spend a whole day in the company of Bristol or Birmingham or Burton-on-Trent, as mile by mile we approached, drew level, and finally left them behind.

We reached Inwardleigh about six. The hoofs of

our four horses made a fine clatter through the village, and children ran out from cottage doors, gazed spell-bound for a moment, and then rushed back to tell their friends and relations that a whole cavalcade was riding by. Dogs flew out barking, and Thos, who was always loudly provocative until the enemy came within striking distance, let out a few shouts of defiance, and then took refuge among the horses' legs. He had already been knocked down and bitten by a carter's collie, but even that had not taught him the folly of challenging strange dogs in their own villages.

By this time I was unaccountably weary, and would have done much to halt at Inwardleigh. But we were still behind our schedule, and had planned to continue at least as far as Lamerton Cross, where we must turn left towards Jacobstowe and Exbourne. Reaching the cross-roads, we began to look hopefully for a farm. When you are well before time and freshly energetic, the land seems crowded with suitable farms, and all you have to do is to make your choice. Whereas if you are late or hungry, or vexed with bad weather, there is never a house in sight. Near Lamerton were fields and woods and cattle, but no sign of farm-house or even of outbuildings, until having proceeded wearily in the direction of Jacobstowe, we spied a substantial farm with large fields ; but alas ! it stood a good six hundred yards back from the road. If they refused us (and in those

early days of inexperience I had less faith in the kindness
of farmers), we should have nearly a mile of extra
travelling, and all perhaps for nothing.

But we were lucky. Near the gate we met a
man in a car who told us that the farmer at West
Risdon (for this was the name of the place) would
certainly give us grazing : and so he did. The field
in which we were quartered was one of the most
attractive sites we found, but a long way from the
yard, and by the time we had finished unpacking it
was nearly dark, for the sky was overcast and the
moon not yet risen. We went to the farm-house
for tea, which, though not as lavish as the feast at
Cookworthy, left us mightily refreshed. I am not a
lover of tea, but never in my life have I drunk so
many gallons as I did on this journey, or found it so
pleasant and reviving. There was no running water
in the field, so we filled our canvas buckets at the
back-door pump and carried them down. Here, as
in most other places, these pails aroused great interest:
how in the world did they hold so much without
leaking ? We also arranged to call in the morning
for boiling water, thus dispensing with the primus,
which was nothing but a nuisance.

The field, which was very large, contained some
good grass, but most of its area was covered by a
thicket of bushes and young trees, with here and
there a marshy pool fringed with reeds and the lush
bog grass beloved of cattle. On our return from

tea, the horses, which we had left grazing by the gate, were nowhere to be seen, and Spencer made a tour of the field to see where they were and inspect the hedges, which in this type of enclosure are not always to be trusted. After a time he came back and reported that the fence was sound and all four horses feeding among the trees. To save space in the tents, we piled the saddlery under a bush and covered it with our waterproofs.

The night was cloudy, dark and very still, without sound of wind or running water. From time to time I heard the hooting of owls, or the noise of horses crashing their way through the tangle of brambles and dry twigs. I was very tired that night — so tired that I began to wonder if I could do the whole journey without some radical change of plan. The shifting of the pack to Martha had put an end to our worry with the load, but Jenny was too wide to be ridden with comfort all day. And there were other troubles. The arrangement by which Joey carried the valise was good in itself, but involved the sacrifice of my comfortable Army saddle, though after the Bodmin Moor disaster it would hardly have been fit for a rider. The other riding-saddle, though very well cut, and liked by everyone else who used it, for some reason or other did not suit my anatomy, and I could not sit on it long without galling. Now a saddle-gall is of small account, if one is not riding every day. But on a long and continuous journey even a slight

sore can become a misery. I had tried the effect of
my waterproof folded into a pad ; and later in the
day I rode and walked in alternate spells. This in
itself is sound, for it rests both horse and rider, but
when one is hampered by a stiff knee, a waterproof
loosely folded, and the rein of a led horse, the constant mounting and dismounting becomes tedious.
Joey had a marked dislike of walking on the inner
or left side of Jenny, and whenever I stopped to dismount, would edge to the right and get his rein
involved with hers. At such critical moments a car
would approach, or Thos, with ill-judged enthusiasm, would bark in front of the horses. Or the waterproof would fall off, or worst of all, the whole saddle,
pulled over by my weight hanging awkwardly on one
stirrup, would slip sideways. All this was sheer un-
handiness and bad riding, but this did not lessen the
tedium and vexation.

Nor had Martha's lot been easy. She carried the
pack with excellent steadiness, but the frequent hills
tried her, and a pack-horse has the disadvantage of
bearing a dead weight which cannot be eased until
the final halt. Jenny was tougher and stronger, and
I suggested to Spencer that we should give her one
more trial with the pack, and see whether, by the
most careful roping and balancing, we could not keep
it in place. On level roads the swaying would be
less ; but though there were no more moors to cross,
Devon is a hilly county and the only comfortable

E

gradients are on those very main roads we wished to avoid. It may sound paradoxical, but if you want easy going in any district that is not quite flat, keep to a mountainous country where the heights are too great to be climbed directly, so that the traveller must follow the rivers or coast-line, and cross the hills by regular passes. It is in rolling country like Devon, where (excluding the moors) the general level does not exceed 1000 feet, that the gradients are so steep, for the hills are not high enough to be insuperable, and all but the most modern road-makers considered it unnecessary, and perhaps poor-spirited, to dodge them.

Next morning we woke to a dismal and steamy drizzle. Grimly we scrapped the large tin kettle, which was an awkward shape to pack, and a few stores that required cooking. We also left behind — needless to say by accident — Spencer's ground-sheet, the loss of which was not discovered till the next camp. The boiling water obtained for our morning tea was a great success, and from this time onwards we always breakfasted on tea, bread and butter, and some kind of cold meat, usually ham. Although I did not call at the house till close on 7 A.M. no one was down, and I had to wait. The west country farmer is not an early riser, unless the arrival of the milk lorry forces him to get up ; and it was not until we reached the Midlands that earlier hours were kept. For the soil of Devon is mostly kind, and will grow crops without

the endless toil required in harsher regions ; so that
the Devon farmer is justified in being at times a
little lazy.

(3) *Wednesday, Sept. 7 — West Risdon to Morchard Bishop*

At 9.20 we moved out of the field.   Although it
was still very close, the rain had cleared, and the
joy of being once more on a narrow and smooth-
paced horse filled me with boundless optimism.   But
my delight was short-lived.   As Jenny rolled out of
Jacobstowe, the pack developed a slight list which
gradually increased until, in the middle of Exbourne
village, she shied at a passing car, and that was the
end.   We hastily led her to the roadside and unpacked.   This was the first time she had shed her
pack in a public place ; it was annoying to remake it
under the eyes of a number of curious bystanders,
especially when we were quite sure that however
well the job was done, the same thing would happen
again, and probably quite soon.   Nor were we mis-
taken.   We had not gone a mile before the ascent of
a steep hill began its work of disintegration.   As the
road was narrow and full of traffic, we anticipated
disaster by leading the horses into a secluded field,
where we could do our work at leisure and undis-
turbed.   While we were busy, Ladybird vanished
through a gap into another field, but I caught her

before she had a chance to roll. We advanced a hundred yards, perhaps less, and then the same thing happened again. This time we hitched all four horses to the railings of a private drive, trusting that the proprietor would not choose that moment to come out with a car.

We had also made an intentional halt in Exbourne to buy corn and provisions, and here, as at Bratton Clovelly, the village shop was excellently stocked. I have now a good working knowledge of country stores from Cornwall to Cumberland, and can divide them into three classes : (*a*) where you can buy cooked ham, meat pies, bananas, and bread ; (*b*) where they sell tinned peas and perhaps tomatoes ; and (*c*) — dreary places these — where there is nothing to be had but tea and Cadbury's chocolate. All over the country the village shops, like other small private businesses, are being crushed out of existence. Motor vans come out from the big towns to take and deliver orders, and the housewife can buy from them more cheaply than she could at home. And if she wants to shop personally, there is a weekly if not a daily bus to take her to town. The village shop must mostly be kept as a hobby, a side line, or a social club, so little can it pay its way as a commercial undertaking.

At Exbourne I bought meat pies and tomatoes, while Spencer was rash enough to ask the way. It is in leaving towns or villages that one is most likely to go astray, and we were given a wrong turning, which led us south of Sampford Courtenay instead of to the north through Bondleigh, and lost us four or five miles on the day's march. This was annoying, for we had made only four or five miles on Sunday, our first day out, and were to lose still more time on Thursday evening and Saturday morning, so that we did not reach Glastonbury till Saturday night, a whole day later than we expected.

There were one or two heavy showers, but otherwise the day was fair with a wild and thundery sky. In the south-west Dartmoor was still visible, inky black and piled with toppling clouds, which towards Moretonhampstead were dissolving in streams of rain. But we were now getting into a drier part of the country, and henceforward, with the exception of a shower at Marshfield and a sharp thunderstorm at Oddington, there was no rain until the last day of September, when I rode through Wharfedale in mackintosh trousers. The dryness was a great boon to us campers, but there is always something to grumble about : in autumn fine weather brings mist which hides the distant country, and heavy dews that drench your tent like rain. Until we reached Hartington there was no real clearness, and this was a loss ; for the slow unfolding of distant views is one of the greatest charms of travel on horseback. You proceed slowly, even dreamily, gathering impressions; you do not often stop for regular sight-seeing, because if you want to get anywhere, you must keep steadily moving ahead. And after a time the labour of mounting and dismounting, of tying up your horse and focusing your camera, becomes incredibly distasteful.

Lunch-time found us in sight of North Tawton. We halted on the south side of the river, where we noticed a small paddock with two or three cows in it. Entering boldly, we piled our baggage in an open shed, and turned the horses loose to graze. The sun was shining fiercely, and the sheltered river valley was hot and airless. We ate our pies in the shade of the hedge, while Thos lay asleep with the saddles in the linhay. We were quite near the town, and many people must have seen us, but no one interfered ; and in this public place we had as peaceful a midday halt as anywhere else on the journey, though we had to water the horses later, as at this point we could not get down to the river. In reloading after lunch the pack-saddle was put on Martha.

The afternoon's ride was rather dull and tiring. The roads we followed from North Tawton through Zeal Monachorum to Morchard Bishop, though not technically major ones, were crowded and very slippery. There were no grass verges, and the high Devonshire banks cut off the view of the country through which we were passing, even had the flow of traffic allowed us leisure to look at it. Even on the hills the air was close and oppressive, and if there was any breeze, it blew from the south-west upon our backs. My saddle gall was not yet healed, and much of the later part of this day's march was done on foot.

Leaving our field, we crossed the long bridge leading over the Taw, and rode through the town, which is mostly on the north bank. The place looked quiet and deserted ; perhaps it was early closing day, as it always seemed to be at any town we chanced to enter. Quick transport and the centralisation of industry have robbed our smaller country towns of movement and prosperity ; most of the time they doze, and only come to life on market days. North Tawton is off the main road, no great distance from Exeter. Our horses' hoofs rang loud in the empty Georgian streets ; children came out and peeped, and that was all.

From the ridge above the town we had our last glimpse of Dartmoor. It was now a long way off, and still half hidden in clouds. We had first seen it on Sunday from Bodmin Moor, a looming mass in the east, and for the last three days it had served to measure our progress. On Monday it was in the south-east still ahead : on Tuesday as we drew abreast, it lay to the south. Now on Wednesday we had it astern in the south-west, and after that we should see it no more. Dartmoor was the largest and most imposing of our landmarks, and its passing the first real milestone of our journey.

My Kingdom for a Horse

We had no more worry with the pack, having more by chance than skill hit off the correct equilibrium. It was also lucky that Martha was carrying the load, for Jenny, who had hitherto been fairly quiet in traffic, began to shy at everything larger than a one-ton lorry, and anything pale in colour. During the trek I had plenty of time to study the reactions of our horses to various kinds of traffic, and found that unusual bulk and conspicuous colour counted for more than speed or noise. Of buses, a double-decker was much more alarming than a single-decker, however large. A small lorry with a trailer was worse than a large lorry without, while a white-painted motor caravan or truck with lime would frighten them much more than a dark-green van or a lorry loaded with coal. The noisiest motor cycle, being small, was better than the most smoothly running motor bus. I also found that a horse expects a fast-moving vehicle to move fast all the time ; if it slows down or stands by the roadside, especially with the engines running, it must have hostile intentions, or at least is something unnatural and therefore dangerous.

We were now approaching the eastern part of Devon, a fertile rolling country of fine mixed farms and cider orchards, with no great beauty beyond the charm of its thatched and whitewashed buildings. The corn was mostly carried, and in some places they had begun to cultivate the stubbles. The rich aftermath was stocked with Devon bullocks and fattening lambs. Cottage gardens were bright with autumn flowers — asters and Michaelmas daisies, sunflowers and dahlias, and trails of nasturtiums. Our progress was watched by old men digging and women at their doors, while two small girls on their way from school accompanied us for some distance, chattering all the time. At last they asked Spencer what we had in the pack. When he replied " Tigers ", they looked at him doubtfully, for modern education breeds scepticism. They walked beside us for another half-mile, and then one of them turned again to Spencer. " Why isn't the lady riding too ? " she asked, watching me plodding ahead between Jenny and Joey. " Because she would rather walk ", I heard him say. " Oh ! " was the incredulous reply ; and after that, seeing that nothing spectacular was going to happen, the two maidens left us.

Near Morchard Road station we crossed the main road to Exeter, which seethed with every kind of traffic, and the relief of turning up a by-road was like that of escaping from a furious gale into a sheltered refuge. The hum and roar and rattle died into the distance, and we plodded on towards the village of Morchard Bishop, near which we should have to spend the night. According to plan we ought to have camped at Puddington, some four miles further on, but the detour by North Tawton had put that out of the question.

My Kingdom for a Horse

Skirting the village behind the church, we emerged on a long and dreary stretch of road. It was now nearly seven, and the only farm in sight was a very smart and forbidding place on the left. Spencer wanted to try it, but I have a foolish horror of rebuff, and suggested that we should turn up a lane on the left, in the hope of finding some humbler and more homely establishment. I devoutly hoped we should find one soon, as we were all very tired, and the heat had made us cross. Before long we saw an eminently suitable field, and beside it a cottage. We found that the field belonged to the owner of the smart farm, and the cottage to one of his men, who thought that the boss would have no objection, but we had better ask. So Spencer rode back on Ladybird, while I stayed behind with the others. So great was the passion of Thos for racing with horses that after a march of twenty miles, which by running about he had doubtless made thirty, he jumped a high gate and dashed after the rider. We had bespoken tea at the cottage, and I stretched myself on a grassy bank, with the reins of all three horses gathered in my hand, and wondered where on earth we should go if that superior farmer turned us away. But he didn't. After what seemed an endless wait, Spencer came back, and we made our camp.

It was dark before we had done, and we were wolfishly hungry. The cottage was a large one and beautifully kept ; a bright fire blazed in the polished

range. Beside it sat the old mother, while a younger
woman, the labourer's wife, set out a plain but
delicious meal of tea, boiled eggs, and bread and
butter. At first the women were rather dour and
silent, but Spencer was full of talk, and entertained
them with tales of the touring Cossacks, who had
recently visited the West and given a marvellous display of horsemanship. This broke the ice, and we
were soon on easy terms. Later the man himself
came in, and the conversation took a more agricultural turn. By this time we were clear of Spencer's
country, and he was no longer sure of finding common
acquaintances ; but his passion for horse and hound
was useful ; for knowing at least the names of most
hunting celebrities south of the Trent, he was always
able to start a connection.

I had brought several books to read, but I need
not have bothered, for by the time the camp work
was over, and we had fed and talked with our hosts,
and worked out to-morrow's route and written up
the diary, it was too late to do more than read a
few pages in one's sleeping-bag before blowing out
the candle. Spencer, who never read anything, was
always urging me to scrap these books, as they were
heavy and awkward to pack ; and at Glastonbury
they were all thrown out except the Penguin edition
of Cherry-Garrard's *Worst Journey in the World*, in two
volumes, which lasted for the whole trek. It had
been recommended by a friend in Scotland as suitable

camp-fire reading, " for ", as he put it, " however bad
your journey may be, it will be better than that
one ". Actually I had read the book before, and
shall often read it again, though the copy I carried in
my rucksack is so tattered and stained with damp
that it will not last very long. I have read nearly
everything that deals with Scott's last expedition, and
its members are more familiar to me than most of
my acquaintances. To open *The Worst Journey* for a
few minutes each night in my sleeping-bag was like
meeting old friends, and I looked forward to this
cheering and friendly ending to a long and often
lonely day.

(4) *Thursday, Sept. 8 — Morchard Bishop to Stoodleigh*

There must have been thunder somewhere, for
during the night the wind shifted suddenly to the
north-east and began to blow hard, with occasional
scuds of rain, which pattered loudly on the fly-sheet
of my tent. Thos was tired, and his weariness bred
resignation. He ceased to despise the tent, in which
he spent a long unbroken night of sleep, remaining
there until the horses were ready for the road, when
he rushed out with his usual joyful and excited barking. The morning was fine with a strong invigorating
wind. The change to cool fresh weather did us much
good, and for the first time we marched ten miles

before lunch. While we were packing the postman appeared. He had heard all about us, and inspected the kit and horses with great interest. There was no charge for the grazing, and we set out in good heart, turning right along a straight and not very interesting road which led through Black Dog to Puddington. Near Black Dog we got involved with some cows, which were being driven at a leisurely pace by a family party crowded into a dilapidated governess cart — the last hint of the West ! This was a region of forward soil and lower rainfall, and most of the corn was already stacked. The bullocks and fat lambs were in excellent order, and the whole country-side looked smiling and prosperous.

At Puddington I enquired for a shop, but the village was small and there was little to be had but chocolate and bully beef. We could not buy corn for the horses, but the excellence of their night and midday grazing made it possible to do without it. In the south of England it is very difficult to obtain oats in summer and autumn except from a regular corn merchant ; and in these days, when the big city firms deliver far and wide by lorry, most of the country millers have disappeared, and the long-distance rider must either carry several days' supply or go without. For in September most farmers are not feeding their horses ; you can sometimes get cake or bran, but often not even that. We had the annoyance of seeing millers' lorries, piled with bags of corn and cake, passing us on the road, while we were unable to buy a few pounds for ourselves. In the North, where the short summer and bad weather compel the farmer to feed his stock more liberally, I had no trouble in getting corn at village stores or at farms where I stopped for the night.

With the prospect of easier roads, we gave Jenny one more trial with the load. The morning march passed without incident, but on the other side of Tiverton we had so much trouble that we never allowed her to carry the pack again, and I was doomed to ride her from Stoodleigh to Hartington, a distance of about 250 miles. Once I was much attached to Jenny, but after that experience I never wished to see her again.

After Puddington, which is about seven miles west of Tiverton, we had to cross ridges, separated by valleys about 300 feet lower. The gradients, especially on minor roads, were sudden and abrupt. We lunched in a delightful grassy lane, where we could turn the horses loose and herd them while we ate. The hedges were full of brambles, and while Spencer unsaddled, I wandered down the lane with one of the pannikins and soon had it filled with blackberries. These, mashed up with a little sugar, made a refreshing finish to a rather dreary meal of bully beef and stale bread. Blackberries are a great boon to the traveller, and we were now at the height of their season. But for some mysterious reason we never saw many, except at times when it was not convenient to pick them.

The afternoon's march was a perfect switchback. We intended to miss Tiverton by half a mile, with a brief halt on the outskirts to allow me to call at the post-office for letters. As it turned out, we might have ridden through the town with ease and comfort, as it was early closing day, and quiet as the grave. We should thus have saved some time, but our policy was to miss all towns, except when it involved a circuit of many miles. At Nethercleave we slithered down an abrupt and stony descent into a combe with a mill at the bottom, and then climbed an equally steep slope to join the main road on the further ridge. Crossing this, we followed another twisting by-road which finally gave us a view of the smoke of Tiverton far below in the valley. We came to the point where the road forked right into the town, and left along the river towards Bampton. The load began to shift, and Spencer wanted a long halt, in which he could repack at leisure. A suitable field was found, and leaving him there I hurried down on foot, for the road was so steep and slippery that a pony would have been more hindrance than help.

The General Post Office was at the further end of the town, and in looking for it I had the annoyance of passing numerous shops with tempting displays of food, but every one of them was closed. A large bundle of letters awaited me, and I spent some time in reading them, and writing postcards in reply. On my way back I gazed wistfully at all the shops, and especially at a window full of pies and various kinds of delicatessen. How wretched it is to have money in your pocket, and a sight of the things you want to buy, and yet be unable to get them ! In the midst of this display I saw a card announcing that the shop, which also supplied light meals, would be open at 5 P.M. I looked at my watch. It was just half-past four. Should I wait another half-hour and buy some pies and other delights ? A most difficult decision. We had a long way to go, and already an hour had passed since I left Spencer with the horses. I decided to go on. My strength of mind was rewarded, for near the bridge I found a small shop open where I bought bananas and some pies which, though not as showy as the others, seemed good enough when we came to eat them.

I pelted back as hard as I could, and arriving hot and breathless at the gate of the field, found Spencer outside with the horses ready to start. But his luck was out. He had just unloaded Jenny, and had all the kit spread out on the grass, when the owner of the field appeared and wrathfully ordered him off. Spencer explained that he was merely adjusting a load that had slipped, but the farmer, who obviously took us for some well-dressed but sinister kind of gipsy, gave him ten minutes to be gone, and most of his wait was spent at the roadside. I was glad that I had not fallen for the delicatessen, and reflected that the nearer one is to civilisation, the less friendly is one's fellow-man. In a solitary place such a reception would be unthinkable.

Another disappointment was in store for us. Where time is important, the crossing of rivers is always a problem, especially when one wishes to avoid towns. The obvious place to cross the Exe was at Tiverton ; but as far as we could gather from the map, there was a bridge near Bolham, about two miles further on, which could be reached by a private road ; and by using this we could make straight for Hockworthy. On further enquiries, we were told that the present owner of the estate had closed the road, and if we wanted to cross, we must either return to Tiverton or proceed to the bridge at Cove Halt. We decided to go on, and the choice was lucky, for the by-road between Tiverton and Cove is one of the prettiest in Devon. The valley of the Exe is charmingly wooded, and as the railway and the main road are both on the opposite bank, there is little traffic to spoil one's enjoyment of the scene. The wind had dropped, and the sky was serene and cloudless. But Jenny was bent on spoiling our pleasure. As she rolled up and down the numerous short hills, the load swayed most devilishly, and every few minutes we had to stop for readjustment. On each ascent the saddle, which naturally tended to slip back to the full extent allowed by the breast-collar, would give a little, so that the girths were pulled backward out of their right position, thus becoming too slack to hold the load in place. This we prevented to some extent by passing the strap of the front girth through one of the forward baggage hooks ; but it was only a palliative, and the rest of that lovely evening was spent in a continuous and wearisome struggle with the pack.

This work fell on Spencer, and by six o'clock he was tired and ready to camp. We saw on the right a small farm with fields running down to the river — a pleasant place, and as far as we could see, quite suitable. But as we had lost some time in failing to cross at Bolham, we decided to go a little further. But Jenny thought otherwise. We had not gone fifty yards before the saddle slipped again ; we turned back to the farm gate, where a man stood watching our approach. We made our usual request for a field to camp in. I did not like his looks, and was not surprised when, after a long and rather insolent stare, he refused. A little further back we saw two men thatching a hayrick. They directed us to another farm, which lay about half a mile up a lateral valley. As the load was not fit to travel even that distance without readjustment, I waited with the horses while Spencer rode on to enquire. This was a tedious halt. Not only was I harassed by uncertainty, but vexed with clouds of midges, which made the horses stamp and toss their heads. Presently Spencer came back with good news, and we proceeded very gingerly, steadying the pack by hand, as it was not worth while to repack. The farm was brand new — in fact they had only been there a few months, and had not yet finished making the garden. A retired farmer with grown-up children had bought some land in this pretty valley, and built himself a house of the garden-city type, with every convenience and ultra-modern decoration. The place looked so superior that I felt shy of asking for tea, but the people had a kindly air, and we were so tired and hungry that the thought of camping unfed was too grim to contemplate. They promised boiled eggs, and while the meal was preparing we pitched our tents in the steepest field that was ever offered. They suggested that we should go down to the level bank of the stream, but we saw a crowd of yearlings there, and nothing is more hindering than a mob of inquisitive cattle. Also the midges would be worse by the water. So after much looking about we found a fairly level pitch beside the upper hedge ; but as we had unloaded near the entrance gate, we had some distance to haul our equipment.

It was now getting late. We left matches and candles at hand in the doorway of the tents, and went towards the house. It stood high on a ledge, and was approached by a steep path with steps, which led through a bald and half-finished rock-garden. The light inside was blinding, and everything glittered with shiny new paint; there were ultra-modern fireplaces and chromium-plated bathroom fittings, and in the midst of all this glory, exiled and forlorn but not without dignity, stood the homely, shabby Victorian furniture of the old farm-house. On the jazz-papered walls hung some antiquated photographs and engravings, including a grim and snowy scene in the Crimea entitled " The Roll Call ".

That night we slept soundly, lulled by the murmur of the stream below. In the bright moonlight we hardly needed candles. By this time I had come to love my tent, and the few things in it — the mattress and sleeping-bag and Army blanket, the enamel candlestick, the pile of kit-bags and saddles, and the tin box marked " Oxo " in which I kept my letters, money, and fountain pen. Here I could retire to live my own life and think my own thoughts, to write my diary and read *The Worst Journey in the World*. My tent was not far from Spencer's, so that I could see his light and ask him the time ; but once the candles were out, I was miles away in spirit, free and alone with the night.

I opened the " Oxo " tin and stored away the letters collected at Tiverton. One contained a cheque for one of the horses sold by private bargain after the sale. It was less than a week ago, and yet all that had happened there seemed incredibly remote. The moon, which had risen above the woods on the further bank of the Exe, flooded the field with its calm impersonal radiance. There was a chill in the air, and the dog lay curled in a tight ball, nose in tail, for the natural creature loves fug. I pulled up the hood of my bag, snuggled well down, and fell asleep.

V

Somerset

(1) *Friday, Sept. 9 — Stoodleigh to Kingston*

It was a cloudless morning, but very cold, with an unusually heavy dew. Emerging from our tents, we found that the sun had not yet risen above the wooded hills on the further banks of the Exe. We longed for a hot drink ; and although pretty sure that our hosts, being sensible people, would be still in bed, I seized the teapot and packet of tea, and ran across the dripping grass towards the house. In the yard I met the old man going out to milk. But as I had feared, the womenfolk were not yet astir ; and leaving the teapot on the doorstep, I returned to the field and started to pack. We got our boiling water later, and took the road at the usual time.

The early brilliance did not last. There was no rain but a good deal of cloud, and the keen north-easterly wind was very cold. We followed the Exe for a couple of miles, and then turned right at Cove, where there is a bridge and level crossing. On the left we noticed a large quarry ; the stone is mostly worked for road repairs. Lorries came and went, and there were a number of overhead trolleys running on cables to the railway siding. The noise could be heard a mile off, and as we drew near it became amazingly loud. I wondered what Jenny would think of it. Oddly enough, she paid not the slightest attention, perhaps because the noise-making agency was not on the road, nor very close beside it.

Crossing the river and railway, we began the long ascent towards Ashbrittle and the Somerset border. As we climbed, we had striking views of the Exe valley, which above Cove runs north and then north-west towards Dulverton, becoming ever narrower and more thickly wooded. We thought how pleasant it would be to follow the stream to its source in the Exmoor hills ; but this would not lead us to Scotland, and not without regret we turned away. There was not much pleasure in riding Jenny, but my galls were better, and the judicious use of a waterproof as a cushion saved me from serious discomfort. And for the last three days of this week, while I still had Joey available, I rode him in the afternoon, and found relief in the change.

The morning march passed without incident. I had bought enough food in Tiverton to last the day, which was lucky, for we passed no shop till afternoon. We lunched in a charming field near Ashbrittle — one of the pleasantest halts of the whole march, though there was a disappointing scarcity of black-berries. The field was approached by a narrow lane which, though muddy and overgrown, revealed at every gap and gateway a beautiful view of the steep ridges and winding valleys of the Devon and Somerset border. Such lanes are a pleasure to the horsemen, though they have their pitfalls, especially for pack-horses. They are mostly inches deep in mud, and overhanging branches and trails of bramble oblige one to duck continually, and keep a sharp eye on the load. In one of these leafy tunnels we were confronted with a wide sheet of water of unknown depth and uncertain bottom. The horses did not like it, and it needed some patience to get them across. The retentive mud on the further side was worse than the water, and after much splashing and floundering, I was relieved to see Martha and her burden once more on dry land.

In the afternoon we crossed the county boundary, and observing on the right a large and prosperous-looking farm, enquired for corn and were lucky enough to get it. A labourer was bringing his tractor back to the yard ; it was one of the first we had seen, and caused a stir among the horses. The farmer and his men were much interested in our expedition, and after some talk we went on our way with a load of oats in front of each saddle.

As we descended the eastern side of the ridge, a fresh view opened before us — the western end of the fertile Vale of Taunton, and beyond it the Black-down Hills. The north-east wind had brought its characteristic haze, and these hills, with the striking Wellington Monument, were only just visible. But the sight of them, like the vanishing of Dartmoor, was a definite milestone, and gave us much pleasure.

There was a fair amount of traffic on the road, and west of Milverton we met a fresh horror — a pair of actively puffing steam-rollers. These machines, so sluggish and harmless, are always alarming to horses, no doubt because they are large and emit white jets of steam or perhaps because their very slowness suggests some evil purpose. There is also the dis-quieting paraphernalia of boards and lamps and bar-riers and heaps of stone and tar-barrels and armies of workmen. The road is up, and if you are not careful, the horses are off as well. As we approached, the drivers shut off steam, and while Spencer urged forward his charges, one of the men assisted me with mine.

After a time we reached Milverton, which like so many large villages consists of one immensely long street. The place itself was quiet, but there was much through traffic, including several large and fast-moving buses. I was then riding Joey. The traffic he disregarded ; but he took a great dislike to a kerb of light-coloured stone which for a good 300 yards bordered the left side of the road. To avoid this, he was constantly trying to edge out into the middle, and our progress was tedious and crablike. He was also much pestered with flies, of which he had always been impatient ; and when they bit him under the belly beyond the reach of his tail, he would dance and kick as if possessed of the devil. At the same time I was leading Jenny, who shied at every bus, so that I was glad to see the last of Milverton.

We climbed another hill, and crossed a stretch of rolling country where we saw Shorthorns as well as Devons — a sign that we had left the mainly beef-producing districts and were approaching the rich dairy land of Somerset. Towards evening we dropped into the plain of Taunton, leaving the town itself on the right and a good four miles away. This was a bad country for camping. The farms were large and far apart, and the fields, compared with the snug enclosures of Devon, seemed of vast size, unsheltered and unfriendly. There is no more unpromising place for a camp than a flat thirty-acre field bounded by ditches or wire fences. Presently we passed a horse-breeding establishment, where, had we known, we should have been well entertained.

Soon after this we emerged upon a busy main road. Such roads are always hateful, but especially at the end of a long day's march, when the unceasing racket and the constant need for vigilance frays your nerves, and doubles the natural weariness of travel. I found it simpler to dismount and lead my horses. We kept a sharp look-out for a suitable place, but none appeared. At last we found a turning which seemed to lead to a farm ; on a closer inspection we saw the roof and chimneys of a house standing in trees, possibly half a mile away. We decided to try it. After opening and closing three or four gates, a tiresome business with led horses — we reached the yard, only to find the house locked up with a noisy dog in charge.

In bitter disappointment we pulled out the map, and in the failing light saw what appeared to be a bridle-path to Kingston village, which passed through the fields at the back of this farm. We opened and closed a few more gates, and rode across a number of large fields, until the tracks we were following grew fainter and finally vanished, leaving us at a dead end. We turned back. By this time the daylight was gone, but the rising moon gave light enough to guide us over these wide and open fields. In one enclosure was a large herd of inquisitive young cattle, who pursued us to the gate and tried to follow the horses, though we slammed the gate in their faces, and Thos was rash enough to bark at them. Whereupon they turned in a body and mobbed him ; and we watched him in ignominious flight across the field, chased by a crowd of indignant bullocks. To find the short cut in the dark seemed hopeless, and we plodded drearily back on our traces. Between the homestead and the main road we met a man who directed us to another farm on the right, which belonged to the same family as the one we had found closed. A light was showing in the window. Guided by this, we made our way across the intervening fields. We got permission to camp, but no tea was forthcoming, as they were expecting friends to supper. This was a blow. We had passed a public-house on the main road, but it was at least a mile away, and the modern innkeeper does not like to be asked for food.

I was resolved to get tea that night, but not being Moses, how ? Then I remembered noticing, as we first came in, a house beyond the farm, and looking in that direction, I spied a light. A stream, sluggish and fairly wide, separated it from the fields in which we were to camp. But while Spencer unpacked, I prospected along the bank till I discovered a long greasy plank bridge. Following the star of hope, I found the door and knocked. It was opened at once by a middle-aged man, and rather timidly I explained that we had lost our way, and did he know of any place where we could get a cup of tea. " Come right away in ", he said, and led me into a pleasant living-room, where he introduced me to his wife. They were educated people who had returned from abroad and taken to farming, and nothing could have been warmer than their welcome. They made me rest by the fire while Mr. W——, who must have been tired by his day's work, went out to look for Spencer and bring him in. Later we sat down to a superb meal, and afterwards spent a long evening at the hearth, talking of farming and music, of books and foreign countries, until we felt glad that we had not been received at the large farm at the end of the lane. Our hosts' cottage was quite new, having been recently built by the landlord to replace the rambling, picturesque, but dilapidated farm-house, which was now used as a store. The buildings had also been modernised ; there was a fine cowshed which housed a small but excellent herd of Shorthorns.

When at last we rose to return to the camp, they made us promise to come back to breakfast, which we did : a sit-down meal at a table was a real luxury, and not to be despised. We crossed the little bridge, and guided by the hawthorns and willows which marked the course of the stream, found our tents, and the saddles piled beneath our waterproofs. The big flat field stretched pale and dewy in the moon-light ; far away by the wire fence we could see the dark shapes of our grazing horses. Luckily for them and for us there was little wind, for the camp was bleak and exposed. The main road to Taunton was not more than 500 yards away, and all night long I heard the drone of traffic. Except in very remote places or in times of heavy snow, there are no quiet nights in England now. Long-distance lorries travel night and day ; and from this time onwards we always heard the noise of traffic, either in detail when the road was near, or more often as a dull continuous roar, like the sound of waves on a rocky coast. So much do we take this endless racket for granted, that any sudden noise, however natural, is ascribed not to

God but to some machine. The other day I was walking in Kerry, a mile or more from the cliffs. The air was very still, and having reached the highest part of the road, I heard a sudden booming sound. " Good heavens," I thought, " there's a powerful lorry coming." It was the sea !

(2) *Saturday, Sept. 10 — Kingston to Glastonbury*

After a splendid breakfast of eggs and bacon, we went in search of the horses. They were still in the field, but at the furthest possible point from the tents. All were easy to catch except Jenny, and she could always be secured if the others were taken first. Mr. W—— came out to show the short cut we had missed the night before. We tried to ford the stream at the nearest place, but the steep, slippery clay banks were impossible for a pack-horse. We crossed by a bridge higher up, and following a track across the fields, emerged upon the road not far from Kingston. Lower Portman Farm, where we had breakfasted, is about four miles from Taunton. The valley, which is bounded by steep wooded hills, is wide and perfectly flat, with a rich soil well suited for dairying and the cultivation of vegetables, and having good towns at hand, many farmers find it worth while to raise market-garden crops. Kingston is an attractive village, with a tall church tower most exquisitely carved. There is also a well-stocked shop, and near it a butcher from whom I bought an enormous bone for Thos.

It was sunny and very hot — the first of five scorching days which were very hard on the horses. There was a long hill out of Kingston, one of the longest and steepest we met, and Jenny, though led, was sweating profusely. I walked ahead, and Spencer, as luck would have it, was following behind with the pack-horse. In settled weather we did not trouble to cover the pack, but carried my ground-sheet folded under the surcingle. At the top of this hill we stopped for a rest, and found the ground-sheet gone. Martha, being slower than Ladybird, always kept well behind, her nose at the leader's tail, and the fall of a lightish object would pass unnoticed. Thinking it must have worked loose on the hill, I rode back to Kingston, but there was no sign of it anywhere, nor had anyone seen or heard of it. After this it seemed better for Spencer to ride in front, so that the pack could be kept under observation. And as usually happens, the precaution prevented the emergency. I rode behind the pack for over 200 miles, and never had anything to pick up.

On the top of the hill was a wide expanse of heath and woodland. In Somerset the ridges are often as poor as the vales are fertile, and this land, though technically enclosed, was little better than open moor. After a while we began to descend. There was a wide view, but the air was too hazy to let us see it all.

My Kingdom for a Horse

Below us lay the valley or rather plain of the Parrett ;
to the left we could see Bridgwater with its shipping,
and in the distance the Polden hills and Glastonbury
Tor. We skirted North Petherwin, and here made
a bad mistake. Wishing to avoid towns, we had
planned to follow the Parrett as far as Huntsham,
where we believed there was a bridge. There was,
but only for trains ; and it would have paid us to
ride through Bridgwater, from which we could have
taken a series of by-roads to Glastonbury. As it was
we had to cross at Burrow Bridge and then trudge
eleven weary miles along a major road. We did
reach Glastonbury that night, but very late, and after
a forced march of twenty-six miles.

By the time we came to Huntsham the heat in the
plain was grilling, and we felt like food and rest.
At the first farm we tried to get corn, but without
success, and at the second we off-saddled and had
lunch. The farmer was an ex-Service man, and took
the greatest interest in the pack-saddle. He was also
impressed by the troop of horses, and supposed we
were going to Glastonbury Fair, which was to be
held on the following Monday. Cheered by the sight
of the Tor, we asked the distance to Glastonbury
and were disgusted to learn that it was seventeen
miles. Actually the Tor is no help, but rather a
hindrance to travellers. The surrounding country is
so flat that this wretched little molehill can be seen
for miles, and rouses hopes as bright as they are false.

Seventeen miles was a very long march for an afternoon, and we packed up as quickly as possible. Nor did the Huntsham paddock tempt us to linger ; it was flat and bare, and the view of tin shacks and main-line railway embankment, with the ceaseless clatter of passing trains, suggested not rural Somerset but the outskirts of an industrial town.

From Huntsham we had a six-mile trek along the river-bank to Burrow Bridge. The Parrett is not a beautiful river. It flows with swift but turbid current between clay banks artificially raised to a safe height, for the adjacent fields are below the level of the stream. These fields, large, lush, and strictly rectangular, divided by drains and full of drowsy Shorthorn and Frisian cows, have an air of Holland or the Fen country, until you lift your eyes to the hills that close the horizon. Our road was no more than a broad towing-path along the top of the dyke, and when we met anything, which luckily was not often, it was difficult to pass without taking the horses very near to the edge of the steep and sticky bank. After an hour of this travel, the road looped away from the river, and did not return till it joined the main road at Burrow Bridge.

This place is surprising and picturesque. Out of the wide and fertile plain rises one of those sudden abrupt hills so characteristic of Somerset. They were camps or strongholds in pagan times, but later were Christianised and used as sites for churches, which, like other high places at home or abroad, are often dedicated to St. Michael. The church at Burrow Bridge, unlike the ruin at Glastonbury Tor, is still in use, and the plain-dwelling Somerset man, who rarely has to walk uphill, must acquire much merit by climbing 300 feet to church — almost as much as the Mayo man when he ascends the holy mountain of Croagh Patrick, which is nearly ten times as high.

There is a toll at Burrow Bridge, and two men were busy holding up cars and collecting the pence. This toll has a curious effect on the traffic stream, rather like the action of rapids on a river. Cars were released from the bridge in jets, and went on their way in disconnected bunches, and it was quite some time before the stream flowed swift and even as before.

This was the largest stretch of major road we were ever unlucky enough to travel, but by no means the nastiest, for as it was Saturday afternoon there was little heavy transport and few commercial vehicles. But the noise was tremendous : for the road between Burrow Bridge and Street is straight and level, and offers to touring cars a splendid chance of speeding. An endless string whizzed by with a rush and a shriek ; and though the horses behaved well enough, the general nervous strain was great, especially when we were trying to make speed. Luckily for us and for himself, Thos had at last learned to keep to the grass

verge. A country dog, he preferred the middle of
the road, and for the first few days would thread his
way through a stream of traffic, heedless and tail
erect, amid shouts and curses and screeching of
brakes, or would stop in front of some advancing
juggernaut, and turn to look at me with a bland
smile, as if seeking approbation for his sang-froid.
But St. Brigid, who is the patron saint of flocks and
herds and perhaps of farm dogs also, must have given
him her protection, though he little deserved it.

Apart from the traffic, there is another revolting
feature of main roads — their cosmopolitan hideous-
ness and vulgarity. It does not matter what district
they cross, what varied and beautiful country lies to
right and left — the roads themselves remain in vile
uniformity. The same shiny black surface with
startling white lines and arrows and letters com-
manding you to STOP or TURN LEFT ; the same
colossal signposts with lettering that suggests that the
nation is rapidly losing its sight or becoming illiterate;
the same flamboyant filling-stations ; the same strident
advertisements ; the same flimsy refreshments shacks;
the same bed-and-breakfast houses ; the same raw
bungalows and mangy poultry farms. These roads
serve many useful purposes, and one of their truest
but least advertised functions is to provide an awful
and graphic warning of our speedy descent to the
hell of international vulgarity.

We were advancing steadily, but could not hope

to reach Glastonbury before 9.30, so I stopped at
Othery to wire to my friends, for they might give us
up and clear away the supper, a thing that did not
bear thinking of. As we entered the village some
wag called out " The Campbells are coming ! " This
cheered me, for in spite of the heat I was feeling
more like the Retreat from Moscow.

The horses were beginning to flag. I trudged the
rest of the way on foot, and Spencer also dismounted
and led his mare. We could do nothing to relieve
poor Martha, who had lost condition on the march
and looked as hollow as a drum. Joey, with his
small load, was bright and fit, and I was looking
forward to handing him over to Penelope in good
order.

The road ran in a dead straight line across a
" moor ", which in Somerset means a tract of marsh
or bog, even when it has been drained and converted
into lush dairy pasture. There was a grass verge,
and then a deep ditch fringed with willows ; and
beyond that mile upon mile of rich green flats, where
herds of Shorthorns and Frisians were grazing or
chewing their cud. The setting sun slanted in level
beams across the plain. In many fields the cows
were being milked in the open. Floats and trolleys
with churns stood at the gate, while the milkers
passed from cow to cow, sitting down to them just
where they happened to be. This placid primitive
scene was in startling contrast with the feverish

activity on the road. Cars hummed, whizzed, and whirred ; brakes screamed and horns tooted. The horses were too tired to think of shying, and I plodded on in a kind of daze, seeing nothing much but the milestones : Glastonbury 8 . . . Glastonbury 7½ . . . Glastonbury 7. . . . We were moving, but it all seemed unreal, like distance measured in a dream.

Presently we left the " moor " and entered the slightly undulating country at the end of the Poldens. The Tor, which had long been invisible, peeped out again, and looked quite near ; but it was pure devilment, and our hopes were dashed by the damnable accuracy of the next milestone, which registered Glastonbury 6. Six miles to Glastonbury, to friends and supper and bowery orchard for the horses ! We halted for a few moments and I let them graze. The sun had set, but the stream of cars flowed unabated. I thought of the question, ultimately without answer, which was posed by an old man whom a well-meaning Government had evacuated from St. Kilda and settled on the mainland. His new home was near the railway line, and as he watched the trains pass, he would ask : " Why do these trains go up to Dingwall every morning ? They only come back again at night."

Before Glastonbury comes Street, and if you want to experience the full bitterness of hope deferred, you will arrive tired, footsore, and hungry at the

beginning of this interminable row of houses, preferably on Saturday night, and walk right through it to
the very end, leading two horses, and watching two
others being led in front of you. Street is a kind of
model village, a hive of Quaker industry and beacon
of Quaker enlightenment. But to-night it was just
what its name suggests — a street, and an infernally
long one at that. Besides the traffic there were hosts
of pedestrians, for though the business part of the
Fair was kept for Monday, the amusement booths and
roundabouts were open on Saturday. We were
much stared at, though a merciful darkness prevented the inhabitants from seeing the details of our
equipment. The moving crowds and dazzling head-
lights excited the horses, who began to dance along
with short steps, like cats on hot bricks.

After a time we heard a fresh uproar. On the
left a Salvation Army band was blowing for dear life ;
and its brazen and inexplicable din brought Jenny
and Joey to a standstill. Seeing them waver, the
bandmaster considerately stopped the music and sub-
stituted a sung hymn, which, though almost as loud
as the brass, appeared to soothe the horses, and they
passed without trouble. A moment later I heard a
familiar voice, and to my intense delight I saw my
friend H. S. S. with his daughter Penelope. She had
lost no time in coming to meet her new pony, whose
arrival had been most ardently longed for. In the
meantime H. S. S., who had his car with him, offered

to buy us some corn, while Penelope helped us to lead the horses for the rest of the way home.

A stream of talk did much to shorten the road, and the blaring terrors of Saturday night made the horses mend their pace. Between the last houses of Street and the first houses of Glastonbury lies a stretch of open road, at the further end of which is the field where they hold the Fair. From this arose a fierce glare of light and a hellish uproar, which made us keep the horses on very short reins. Goaded by excitement, they walked up Glastonbury High Street at a pace never equalled before or after. Another hill was climbed, and close under the elusive Tor we came to the orchard which was to be Joey's home, and a week-end Paradise for the others. By this time H. S. S. had arrived in his car, and the lights were left on to illuminate the orchard, where we unpacked and fed the horses.

Glastonbury Tor was a major milestone. We had been travelling for seven days, and had covered about 125 miles — a short day's run in a car, but for us an achievement to be proud of.

(3) *Glastonbury Interlude*

At supper (a glorious one) we were asked for travellers' tales, and warmed by food and welcome, we succeeded in making tolerable silk purses out of sows' ears. Later, we pitched our tents on the lawn beside the house, which being half-way up the Tor, commanded a view of the town and the plain beyond it. We might have been camping on the rim of hell. The valley was filled with a harsh glare of light, as if reflected from molten lava in the crater of a volcano. The swing-boats, roundabouts, and other instruments of pleasure, driven by steam or electricity, let out an infernal chorus of groans, clankings, and howls, which, mingled with the hubbub of the crowd, offered a grimly realistic foretaste of the torments of the damned. This went on till long after midnight, when the citizens, sated with noise, went home to bed, and a fog rising from the marshes wrapped us in white appeasing silence.

On Sunday morning we had a long luxurious rest in our bags, followed by a late and opulent breakfast. As we were staying a second night, the tents were left standing, and our only attempt at packing or tidying-up was to cram the junk inside and let down the door-flaps. Then we began to talk about plans. Jenny's shoes were worn to mere slithers of metal, bright as crescent moons, and must be replaced before she went further. The cavalry saddle must be repaired professionally, and this, according to Spencer, would take several hours. We must buy a new ground-sheet and try to reduce our baggage, for we should no longer have Joey to act as auxiliary pack-horse.

Most serious of all was the question of horses.

We were both agreed that Martha would never carry the pack to Scotland. Sooner or later she must be replaced, and the Fair, at which many horses changed hands, offered a chance that might not occur again. We would try to get a better cob, and offer the poor old mare in part exchange. Then we discussed routes. The problem was how to avoid the Black Country and the Potteries. According to the plan worked out at Newton, we must keep as far west as we could without touching Bristol, cross the Severn at Newnham, and leaving the Malvern Hills on the right, pass through East Hereford into Shropshire. South of Shrewsbury we intended to turn east and make our way through North Staffordshire to Ashbourne in Derbyshire. This route was worked out from maps alone, for we had no personal knowledge of this region. But when we described it to H. S. S., who knew the country, he pointed out a number of snags. Our line of march was not sufficiently direct ; and even if we succeeded in dodging Wolverhampton, we were bound to get involved in the Potteries or in the Staffordshire coalfield. He advised us to skirt Bath and cross the Cotswolds to Moreton-in-Marsh. From there we could go to Warwick, and passing between Birmingham and Coventry, cross the Trent near Burton, and make for Ashbourne. He assured us that in following this route we should miss all collieries, potteries, and other horrors, and travel on rural by-roads all the time. We took his advice, and did not regret it. We had, however, to scrap three sheets of the Ordnance map, and as the necessary 1-inch sheets could not be procured locally, we were forced to plan the next few marches from a $\frac{1}{4}$-inch map of the Midlands presented us by H. S. S.

After a traditional Sunday dinner, I retired to my tent to make up some arrears of sleep, while Spencer had sufficient energy to play several sets of tennis. He also gave Penelope some instruction in grooming and harness-cleaning. The orchard, which the horses shared with three or four Guernsey cows, was thick with beautiful grass, but it was so steep that the animals moved like flies on a wall.

Next morning we went to the Fair. It was hotter than ever, and as my breeches seemed unbearably stuffy to walk about in, I got the loan of a skirt. Spencer had already taken Jenny to the blacksmith, and on our way to the Fair ground we left the saddle to be mended, and bought the only ground-sheet in Glastonbury. It was not very good, but larger than those we had lost, so that we could cut it in half and divide it between us.

The Fair opened with a show of mares and foals. When this was over (and it lasted a very long time), we wandered round, inspecting the various horses offered for sale. The only possible cob was a dark bay gelding, about ten years old with a good shape and a quiet eye. We had him out on the road for a trial. He was an awkward trotter, but for a pack-

horse this was of small account, and as he seemed
not altogether unsuitable, we brought Martha into
the discussion. There was, we said, a mare that
we wished to dispose of, and unless she were taken
in part payment, we could not consider the deal.
Martha was still in the orchard, and the owner of the
cob had his motor so deeply embedded in the car
park that it could not be shifted without moving a
dozen others. We took him on foot and at full speed,
and when he reached the orchard he was too hot and
dusty to appreciate Martha's refined and elderly
charm. However, after a lengthy discussion he
agreed to take her in part payment. And while
Spencer led her down to the Fair ground, I cashed
one of my precious travellers' warrants to pay the
difference. I was offered a drink, which on this
droughty day would have been more than acceptable,
but as it was now one o'clock and we had arranged
to meet H. S. S. at 12.30, I was forced to decline.
The arrival of the new gelding, which we called
Excalibur, made quite a flutter among the mares,
and Joey was intensely jealous. But Excalibur, who
was always completely indifferent to company and
surroundings, at once settled down to graze, without
a glance to left or right.

At this point I should have visited the Abbey,
which I have never seen. But some perverse snobbery, or obscure psychological kink, or what you
will, makes me dislike sightseeing ; and this stupid

vandalistic prejudice nearly lost me Killarney, which even when Tom Moore and the Americans have done their worst, remains one of the loveliest places on earth. Yet I believe that few, very few people, if they are honest with themselves, wholeheartedly enjoy sightseeing in itself and for itself. How many of us would do it if no one else did it, and if it cost us nothing ? The trouble is that this activity is nearly always accompanied by horrible physical discomfort. Who has not gazed at Old Masters in icy Florentine galleries, with feet of lead and a drip at the end of his nose, longing all the time for a cup of scalding coffee, or a chance to join the shivering custodian at his wretched brazier ? Or stared at fretted vaults and frescoed ceilings until he wondered if his neck would ever come straight again ? No, I thought, I will not go to the Abbey, nor as a matter of fact did H. S. S. suggest it. Instead he took me to the factory where they make sheepskin slippers, no doubt to warm the feet of Arthurian pilgrims. Here I saw sights of a different kind — skins waiting to be washed, skins dressed, skins dyed, skins half made up into various articles of comfort. In the end I had a pile of cured but undyed specimens thrown down before me from which I was to choose a saddle pad. I selected a small close-wooled skin, very soft and supple ; and when I got it home, I trimmed it to the shape of the saddle and cut slits for fastenings. Thus it was easily detached, and like the upper seats of old-fashioned buses, could be reversed in wet weather.

In the afternoon I bought a collar, chain, and muzzle for Thos, and took him to the train. In the town it was hotter than ever, and the streets were thronged with huge crowds, through which I fought my way to the station. Our progress was slow, for the poor dog, lost in a forest of strange legs, was constantly attaching himself to the wrong pair. I was glad to see him go, for he had had enough of the road. But it took him two days to reach Strome-ferry in Ross-shire, and I have no doubt that long before the end he was wishing himself back with the horses.

Later we tackled the problem of packing. We scrapped one kit-bag full of superfluities, which left us with two valises, two kit-bags, and the light Fish Meal sack. This was a fair load for the pack-saddle, but at that time it seemed an irreducible minimum. Then it occurred to us that if we scrapped one of the kit-bags and stowed its contents in two rucksacks which we could carry ourselves, the pack would be lighter and less awkward. H. S. S. lent us two of his own which had seen war service, and these we filled with the contents of the white kit-bag.

In the evening H. S. S. took me for a run in his car, and we explored the first few miles of the route proposed for the next day. I was not greatly looking forward to the trek through the Midlands, though it proved to be more interesting than I expected, and as we had no further trouble with the pack, a good deal less wearisome.

(4) *Tuesday, Sept. 13 — Glastonbury to Farmborough*

Tuesday morning was misty and still, with a promise of heat to come. Joey was left alone in the orchard, and we started at the usual time, with most of the family to see us off. Penelope had gone to work, otherwise she would have ridden with us for a time on her new pony. We turned down a lane, which missed the centre of Glastonbury and joined the main road just outside the town. Here we met a new horror of the roads — an ironmonger's van. The inside was stacked with more perishable goods, while the outside was festooned with kettles, sauce-pans, colanders, brushes, dustpans, and I know not what else, all rattling and jingling with the motion, like a Victorian lady's chatelaine. It was standing when we passed, and for some time I was waiting for it to overtake us ; but it must have gone another way, for we never saw it again.

For a couple of miles we marched along the main road to Wells, and then turned right, following a grassy track across the " moor " in the direction of Dulcote and Dinder. The scene was much the same as on Saturday — lush fields, willows, and grazing cows — but it had lost much charm ; for to-day there was neither colour nor distance, and both Mendip and Polden hills were hidden in mist.

For me, at least, to-day's riding was much more pleasant. I had no horse to lead and no dog to look after, and the cavalry saddle with sheep-skin pad made a comfortable if not very professional seat. For some reason or other, perhaps because she had no Joey to impress, Jenny began to snail along at the speed of an ox-cart, until I stopped and cut a willow switch, when she promptly mended her pace. A good horse does not need a stick, and I suppose that crops are carried only to open gates or for the sake of a smart appearance. But the average farm beast, whether horse or cow, never respects you without this symbol of authority. This was specially true of Joey, who might slug along with an empty-handed rider ; but the moment you broke a twig from the hedge or a withered foxglove stem from a bank, off he would go with a bang, and as long as you kept the gewgaw in your hand, would never relax his speed. This practice may be unorthodox, but with farm-bred horses it works, and on a long-distance ride it is less trouble to be a pragmatist.

Leaving the " moor ", we climbed into the rolling strip of country at the foot of Mendip. The mist lifted, and we had a glimpse of Wells about two miles to the west — a not very flattering view in which the gasometer was more prominent than the cathedral.

The Tor of Glastonbury had also disclosed itself, but falsely as ever, for the misty air gave it a look of remoteness that flattered our progress. At Dulcote there is a large quarry, and the cliff-like gash in the hill makes an impressive landmark, visible for miles across the plain. Turning right, we passed through Dinder, a small village among trees, with a rather inadequate shop, where I bought a " C quality " lunch.

Our next objective was Maesbury station. The new route, which would lead us through the out-skirts of Bath, obliged us to cross the Mendip hills at the eastern and less interesting end. Wells and Cheddar gorge I had seen before, but I longed for a sight of the bare limestone heights above, with stone walls and sheep and bracing winds and wide views, if only for an hour or two, for south of Ashbourne we had little of this to hope for.

Leaving Dinder, we turned right and began to climb. The hill was long rather than steep, but by now the sun was out, and the air close and oppressive. The horses were sweating profusely, and we had to give them frequent spells of rest. The rucksacks were an unqualified nuisance. They relieved the pack-horse at the expense of both riders and mounts ; the straps cut our shoulders and obliged me to wear a superfluous coat to lessen the friction. My clumsy efforts to mount were not improved by the wretched thing, which would swing forward at the critical moment, upsetting the balance, or catching the arched

front of the saddle. My black curse on all baggage!
No more long trail for me, except with a donkey-
cart or an army of native porters. The road wound
ever uphill, playing a kind of hide-and-seek with a
single-track railway line, which for the most part
runs modestly hidden in cuttings. Spencer thought
that this line might connect Wells with Bristol via
Shepton Mallet, thus bringing a few secluded Mendip
hamlets into the swim of modern progress. But we
were too lazy to work it out on the map, and I still
know nothing about these trains, whose laboured
puffing broke the silence of an empty land.

According to our usual and very sensible practice,
we did not stop for lunch till we reached the highest
point of the road near Maesbury station. Even at this
height it was very hot, and we turned with relief into
a short field lane, closed at the further end by a gate
where we could let the horses loose and keep them
from straying by sitting ourselves at the nearer end.
Once more Providence was kind and sent a few blackberries to sweeten the bitter taste of a " C shop "
lunch. We were very thirsty, and got a good drink
of water at a cottage. The turning-on of the tap
made a sudden gush which scared Jenny, and she
tried to bolt before I got the glass in my hand. I
should have liked some cider, having a passion for
the kind provided in Somerset inns ; but Spencer
thought that fermented drinks were bad to ride on,
in which he may have been right. And as I did not

care to go into a pub and leave him outside, I reluctantly abstained.

Further on we came to another quarry which, like the one we had seen at Cove, provided metalling for the roads. We heard blasting at no great distance, and as we were constantly meeting lorries loaded with broken stone, I concluded that this was not the only specimen. Apart from quarries, the district seemed quiet and thinly populated. We had left behind the scenery most characteristic of Somerset — wide fen-like plains broken by hills abrupt and startling, with a tower or a clump of trees on the summit, and were moving through continuously rolling country, which, as we approached Bath, became steeper and more varied. At this eastern end of the Mendips I noticed neat and most attractive hayricks, of a kind I have never seen anywhere else. They are rectangular, with flattened gables, as in many other places ; but the walls, from the edge of the eaves to the ground, are symmetrically tapered and then trimmed with shears. Much skill and judgment must go to this trimming and tapering, as no doubt it is done without measurement.

This rustic peace did not last for very long. We were not much more than twelve miles from Bristol, and a large town spreads like the plague, especially when some natural barrier, like the sea, forces a one-sided development. In studying the maps at Newton, I wondered if we should be able to slip

between Bath and Bristol without getting involved
with industry or suburbs. We nearly escaped, but
not quite. Here and there we struck blisters of raw
new houses, and here and there some startling and
isolated collieries. We had to ride the full length
of Chilcompton, a semi-residential, semi-industrial
village which is rather less urban, but nearly as long
as Street. The industrial touch is given by a neighbouring colliery, while the Benedictine Abbey of
Downside attracts a great many middle-class residents.

We were half-way through Chilcompton when
Jenny started one of her capers. Our clattering progress down a village street always seemed to coincide
with that blessed moment when school doors open
and streams of children pour forth to find amusement on their devious way home to tea. Horses are
a sure draw, and we soon had a large though orderly
following. The bolder spirits were walking abreast,
so as to be near the pack-horse — a rarer and more
exciting object than either of the saddle horses.
One urchin was close by my stirrup, though he
was far too shy to speak unless first spoken to. He
answered a few questions and then fell silent. But
he must have made some sudden movement, for
Jenny swerved violently into the middle of the road,
where she narrowly escaped a collision with an oncoming car. This was a splendid thrill for the children, and they were still more entertained when
the saddle, complete with sheep-skin, blanket, and

waterproof strapped to the front, slipped to the near side, and I was forced to dismount, loosen girths, remove saddle and blanket, refold and spread blanket, replace saddle without wrinkling blanket, do up the girths, and finally mount without being overbalanced by the swing of the rucksack, or causing the saddle to slip inwards through keeping my weight too long on the near stirrup. This drama was watched by the children with intense interest but quite without mockery ; for all they knew, it might be a regular part of the show ; while poor Spencer looked on with the would-be detached air of one who hopes that nobody is associating him with so much ineptitude.

Leaving Chilcompton, we crossed a valley and began the long ascent to Timsbury, which stands high on a ridge. It was cooler now, but the horses were still inclined to sweat, and on the hills we did a good deal of walking. Excalibur was quite a success. The pack-saddle fitted him as well as it had fitted Martha, and he had the same steady unswaying walk. He was also dead quiet in traffic. But nothing would induce him to come abreast of the leader, and Spencer gave him a long rein, so that he could walk immediately behind Ladybird. Jenny and I brought up the rear. This was a good position, for I could watch the pack, whose looming bulk prevented Jenny from seeing too much of oncoming traffic.

From Timsbury it was a short two miles to Farm-

borough, near which we had planned to spend the
night. The $\frac{1}{4}$-inch map was adequate, but much less
handy to use than the more detailed sheets, which
showed bridle-paths and individual farms, and gave
us the cheering illusion of having covered in our
twenty-mile march an imposing extent of country.

Near Farmborough we came to a pleasant-looking
small farm, at which we asked for grazing. After
watering the horses in the yard, we were led across
the road and up a leafy lane. My wretched saddle
was slipping again, and while Spencer and the farmer
went on with the other horses, I progressed a few
yards at a time, keeping it in position by hand, as we
were too near the journey's end to bother with any
further adjustments. Needless to say, the fault was
not in the saddle but in Jenny's figure, for when I
used it on Ladybird there was no more slipping.

The field was sheltered, secluded, and full of good
grass. We pitched our tents in an angle of the hedge,
and it was well we did so, for in the night it blew
hard from the south-west. When I unrolled my tent,
an earwig, which must have travelled with us from
Glastonbury, emerged from the apex. So far we had
been fairly free of insects ; but through Somerset
and Gloucestershire we were pestered with flies,
moths, earwigs, and daddies, and my evening spell
of reading was always broken by insect hunts.

We went to the farm for tea. It was a simple
homely place, and our hosts were middle-aged people,

in that happy state of semi-retirement when one rears calves and milks a cow or two for the house. They had an orchard, but the apple crop had been spoilt by frost. The wife was charming, dark, and soft-voiced as an Irishwoman, and with a very pretty wit. She told us that when we first came to the door she was loth to take us in, as she was a homekeeping woman, and never quite trusted strangers. But now she was glad to have overcome her scruples. We talked for some time, first on the usual farming topics, and then on the possibility of war. At Glastonbury H. S. S. had, as he put it, been "feeling for his sword", and Spencer, who had served with the Territorials, was wondering whether he would be called up before we reached our goal. However, we reflected that if we were wanted we should soon be found, and having got so far, we might as well go on.

That night the horses, for the sake of shelter, kept close to the tents. In lulls of the wind we heard the steady industrious sound of cropping, sometimes quite close to my ear, until a gathering blast in the trees, and the thunderous flapping of canvas, would drown the friendly sound. I remember reading in *Tschiffely's Ride* that in wild unfenced country he did not need to tether his horses at night, because they never strayed far from the place where their rider slept, as if seeking protection and company ; and by day, his pack-horse followed without a leading rein. Even on our short journey we found that, as soon as the horses were well away from their home surroundings, they kept near the tents, and never tried to break out of the fields, though many of them were badly fenced. But we never risked the ultimate test of camping on moors or on commons.

Next morning, when I went for boiling water, I found the farmer milking, and a neighbour or two at the cowshed door with jugs and cans, waiting to be served with milk. I noticed an old car in the yard, and the farmer told me that he did not keep a horse, but used the car for sweeping and carrying hay, and for most of the carting jobs on the farm. There was a nice-looking float in one of the sheds, which he offered to sell. It would have suited Excalibur, and I was so sick of Jenny's capers that I would have bought it to carry myself and the pack, had I known of someone to take my precious mare. As luck would have it, I got an unforeseen offer the following day, but it was then too late to return to Farmborough for the float. So Jenny was kept.

VI

Gloucestershire

(1) *Wednesday, Sept. 14 — Farmborough to Marshfield*

WE woke to a cloudy morning, with the wind still blowing freshly from the south-west. The hot spell had broken, and we set out in good heart. The country round Bath is quite charming, and anyone who wishes to settle in a district which is hilly without being bleak, and rural without remoteness, should make a point of seeing it. The sheltered valleys and wooded hills are full of dignified Georgian houses and mansions, which stand among trees whose very style of growing has an eighteenth-century spaciousness and calm. The stone-built farms and villages are as attractive as anything in the Cotswolds, while the soil is more fertile and the climate much less severe.

We wandered along at a leisurely pace through leafy by-roads, unvexed by any traffic. The trees and hedges were still thick and green, apples and pears were ripening, and the cottage gardens ablaze with autumn flowers. The only thing we could find to grumble about was the steepness and frequency of the hills, which exceeded any on the whole trek, except those I met in the West Riding between Holmbridge and Mytholmroyd. Our plan was to leave the centre of Bath on the right, and merely skirt the western suburbs on our way to Lansdown. There was no village directly on the route ; and our best chance of buying provisions was at Newton St. Loe, which lay about half a mile to the left of our road.

There were two approaches to this village. When we reached the first turning, I suggested that Spencer should take Ladybird and Excalibur to the second one, and there wait, while I went alone to buy provisions and if possible corn. No sooner clear of the others than I touched up Jenny, and we entered the place at a smart trot — a great relief after so many miles of walking. Newton St. Loe is one of the most beautiful and unspoilt of Somerset villages, being built of stone in a style which is as simple as it is harmonious. Seeing on my left a large farm, with a stackyard full of opulent ricks, I turned in to look for corn. The place was empty, but the clatter of Jenny's hoofs brought out the farmer's wife, who with her daughter was feeding poultry. They had no oats, but offered a mixture of bran and flaked maize, which I accepted. While the girl was weighing the corn, her mother began to admire the mare, and finally asked if she were for sale. I should have made a deal on the spot, for the chance was never offered again. But the difficulty of replacing Jenny weighed on my mind, and I had not yet seriously considered putting Excalibur into harness, which would have been the obvious solution. In the course of conversation the farmer's wife discovered that we had other horses, and concluded that we must be itinerant dealers. When I explained that we were just farmers riding to Scotland, her amazement knew no bounds. We had some discussion about the price of the fodder, and I think I paid too much for it. At any rate Spencer always seemed to get it cheaper, and in future I made him buy the horses' food while I bought ours.

I asked the way to the shop, which was excellent and well-stocked. Being now laden with 25 lb. of bran and maize, and a large bulging brown-paper parcel, I returned more slowly than I had come. Arriving at the cross-roads I was puzzled to see no trace of Spencer and the horses. The map was in his pocket, and I had no idea in which direction to look. Dumping the corn and provisions just inside a field gate, I held up a car, and hearing that the driver had not passed a young man with horses, I turned in the opposite direction and found him at another cross-road further back. We turned, picked up the provisions and rode down a long hill, and then followed a lane across some fields, which soon brought us out upon the main road about a mile outside Bath.

This was a horrible road and very crowded. We crossed the Avon (another landmark) by an exceedingly slippery bridge. On the further side of the river the road became suddenly urban, and featured (the word fits the context) a side-walk edged with concrete, and a tram-line with overhead wires. I had no idea that Bath had trams, and still less idea what the horses would do if they met one. I was soon to discover.

I knew that we had not far to go along this road before turning left to Lansdown, and if the trams were not very frequent we might be lucky enough to escape without seeing one at all. Cars flew past, and lorries and vans, but still no tram, and I was just congratulating myself on our good fortune, when in the open space left by a lull in other traffic I saw the monster approach. It was a double-decker, humming horribly, and as it advanced on us it pitched and swayed like a ship in a swell. I dismounted and led Jenny on to the side-walk, thankful that there was no Joey or Thos to cope with. Jenny gave it one look, turned right about and bolted, dragging me after her. Ladybird, with Spencer on her back, followed suit, towing the unwilling Excalibur, who never allowed himself to be hurried, whether by trams or anything else. Seeing the stampede, the driver stopped and came to investigate. By this time we had checked the horses, and to our surprise the man apologised. We explained that ours were raw country ponies who had never seen a tram ; and having ascertained that nothing was broken, and the pack in good order, we went on our way, and in a few minutes were safely set on the long ascent to the summit of Lansdown. I hear that there is a proposal to abolish these trams and replace them with motor buses. If this is done, I for one shall not be sorry.

We saw no more of Bath, and found but little trace of its influence except in the matter of milestones. Whatever authority is responsible for their lettering has chosen to use Roman numerals ; and such antiquarian snobbery was rather annoying, for Bath II looked very like Bath 11, and suggested that by some miraculous means we had travelled a very long way in a very short time.

Lansdown is a long hill, and it was past lunch-time when we reached the top. Luckily the weather was much cooler, with a fresh breeze that on the summits of hills was almost too strong for enjoyment. Near the golf-links we turned left, following a straight and level road with broad grass verges. We looked about for a sheltered place to halt, but perceived nothing but stone walls and short grass, and the wintry soughing of wind in scattered trees. Clearly there was to be no lunch till we had dropped some distance on the other side. Presently we turned right and began to descend towards Langridge. The road became narrower and more wooded, and after a while we saw a gap in the hedge, which led into a small enclosure, much overgrown with furze and brambles. Here there was shelter, and grass of a sort. We led the horses through the gap and began to unpack.

Spencer had just finished unsaddling, and I had our provisions all spread on the ground, when we heard a shout, followed by the sudden appearance of an angry face on the other side of the hedge. " Clear out of here ! " I heard the fellow say, and wearily began to gather the mugs and pannikins. Another Tiverton, I thought, and we were so hungry ! Spencer rose to explain that this little corner was open to the road, and in any case, was waste land. But the explanation was unnecessary. As soon as the farmer saw our moderately respectable clothes and extremely respectable saddlery, he was all smiles and apologies. " I saw the 'osses," he said, " and thought you was gipsies." And he plunged into a diatribe against the nasty habits of nomadic people. Ladybird and Jenny need not have resented the mistake, for whatever may be wrong with gipsies, their horses are always good.

After lunch we crossed the Langridge valley and climbed another long hill, which led to a windy ridge, covered with stubble and not much lower than Lansdown. We paused for a rest beside an enormous rick of corn, so deeply undercut that it seemed to sway in the wind. The sky was full of hurrying grey clouds which threatened rain, but none fell. Another couple of miles brought us to the hamlet of Cold Ashton, where there is an old church and a most beautiful stone manor-house with terraces and wrought-iron gates, built to command a view down the last wooded valley on the south-western edge of the Cotswold plateau.

Half a mile further on we turned right towards Marshfield. We were riding on the main road to Chippenham, as usual hideous with traffic ; but the switchback hills had driven the devil out of Jenny, and she plodded quietly along the grass verge as if the vans and lorries had been so many sheep or cows. Marshfield is another of those beautiful deserted little towns where almost every house is a perfect specimen of Georgian or Queen Anne architecture, and had they not been strung out along a major road like pearls threaded on galvanised wire, our passage would have been sheer delight.

On the further side of Marshfield the road became worse, as for many hundreds of yards it was under repair, so that all the traffic was concentrated on one side. The surrounding country was flat but high, about 500 feet above the sea, and a chilly wind was whistling over it. Presently we turned left along a quiet empty by-road, and began to look for a place to camp. The sky grew suddenly dark, and a smart shower came down — just enough to make me un-strap the waterproof and turn my sheep-skin, for I was now on foot. We spied a large farm-house on the left, standing well back from the road in a broad enclosure of roughish grass. Leaving Spencer with the horses, I went in to ask for grazing.

The door had a bell, and as we were now in an

Anglo-Saxon country, it rang, and loudly too. It was answered by an old woman as deaf as a post. At last I succeeded in making her understand. She said that the large paddock on the other side of the road would be a good place, but there were pigs in it, and if we would ask her son, who lived in a cottage dimly visible in a clump of trees, he would no doubt shut up the pigs, and we could camp there. Yes, she would make us some tea, but we had better see about the pigs first. I quite agreed with her, for pigs are capable of anything, and Spencer had some grim tales of tents wrecked and provisions devoured.

I found the young man, and he came back with me to show us the way to the field. It proved to be a big place, about 300 yards in length, well sheltered with trees and bushes. It would not be easy, he said, to shut up the pigs, as he had no house for them ; but as there were only three, and they always stayed at the end where he fed them, we were not likely to be troubled, especially after dark. So we risked the pigs, and camped. Ladybird and Excalibur were unloaded first, and turned loose. This flouting of seniority offended Jenny, who showed her annoyance by deliberately breaking the strap of her night-halter with a jerk of the head — a trick well known to her.

While we were busy unpacking, the farmer came out and looked at the horses with great interest. He was a fine old man in the later sixties, with jet-black hair and humorous dark eyes. He examined our gear and asked a good many questions, and then led us back to the house, where tea was set in the large and comfortable kitchen. The old lady was there, and two of the grandchildren. Their eldest sister was married, and our black-haired host already a great-grandfather. He talked of the old times, and said that in his youth the labourers were far more contented with their small wages than they were to-day, when they earned double the amount : for now the farmers were too hard up to give them any perquisites and extras. The land round Marshfield was poor, and needed the treading and dunging of folded sheep ; but nobody now could afford the labour. He plied us with cider and port, and it was late before we left the cheerful fire and went in search of our tents.

The night was dark and we had no torch. We lost our way in the huge enclosure round the farm, and it was some time before we found the gate of the camping field. Here the gloom was increased by the clumps of trees and bushes, and we stumbled about in the long wet grass, tripping over trails of brambles and hidden stumps and roots. At last we saw the glimmer of canvas, and while I groped for matches and candle, Spencer went to locate the horses.

During the night the wind veered north, and we woke to a bitterly cold morning. It was a long way to go for boiling water, and by the time I got back to the tents, the tea was well stewed. The old couple refused any payment for grazing or tea, so we tipped the children, and departed with good wishes from everyone.

(2) *Thursday, Sept. 15 — Marshfield to Cherington*

The morning, though cold, was brilliantly fine, and we marched steadily across the plateau in the direction of Tetbury, where our letters were waiting. On the previous day we had crossed the Somerset-Gloucester boundary, though I am not sure of the exact point. To-day we were to step into Wiltshire and out again, and after that it was all Gloucestershire till we reached the Four Counties Stone near Moreton-in-Marsh.

The first part of the morning's ride was easy but monotonous. The land is rather poor, and largely devoted to corn-growing, though the flocks of folded sheep that were once the making of this country are now conspicuous by their absence. We travelled on level roads between wide empty fields, fenced with stone walls. Trees were few and poorly grown, and homesteads widely scattered, for it would take many acres of such land to make a sizable farm. The south-western counties had largely escaped the drought of 1938, but here, on porous limestone, the ravages of a dry summer were very noticeable. Hayricks were small, pastures thin and bare, and the only note of colour was the rich gold of newly stacked corn and the tawny bloom of stubbles. We were now remote from main thoroughfares, and free from the everlasting din of traffic. But in modern England there is no peace for tired ears. No sooner do the lorries and the vans depart than the air is full of the persistent, far-reaching drone of aeroplanes. Owing to its central position and level open spaces, the Cotswolds have become a favourite site for aerodromes, and anyone who looks for quiet should go elsewhere.

Presently, by one of those sudden changes of scenery that so pleasantly diversified our journey, we came to the beautifully wooded country round Badminton. This was England of the mansions and the big trees, remote alike from aggressive industry, trade unionism or agricultural depression. In such a place Dukes must be Dukes indeed, with coronets and plenty of cash, and not penurious exiles or outmoded lay figures. In the neat village at the Park gates there must still be people who would recognise the gentry when they saw them, and old women who would curtsey and dust you a chair to sit on. No one here would think of taking the *Daily Herald*, even to light the fire, and the name of Maxton be too little known to provoke as much as a smile.

We learnt that we could ride across the Park, and save some distance on the way to Tetbury. A very old man, with an authentic but rather difficult dialect full of z's, directed us to the big gate, which was thrown open by a small boy, to whom Spencer, for the glory of our saddles and bridles, gave a tip. Though when I looked at the shabby kit-bags, and remembered my own battered linen hat, I felt that we were more in a position to receive tips than to give them. The wide expanse of the Park, with its groups of well-chosen and carefully planted trees, and a big herd of cattle grazing in the distance, was a great delight and refreshment. No cars, no lorries, no people, nothing but grass and woodland. What a place for a gallop, if only Excalibur with our miserable baggage were left behind ! The poor patient beast looked ugly, superfluous, and utterly plebeian. He was a nice-looking horse when loose in the field ; but as shabby ill-fitting clothes will spoil a handsome man, so Excalibur was degraded by the burden and trappings of a nomad. His dark amiable face was shadowed by over-large blinkers, decorated with tarnished brass discs, which stared vacantly like the eyes of dead fish, and the bulging pack, covered by one half of the new but shoddy ground-sheet, gave him the look of a misshapen camel.

We trekked in silence across the Park, and at the far end found another gate, but without an urchin to open it. It was one of those massive swing gates that you push open, dash through, and allow to clang behind, and with a horse you must be very prompt indeed. Turning right, we marched along a quiet shady road, with dense woods on either side. Here and there were straight grassy rides, which offered long and seductive views of tree-trunks in diminishing perspective. This pleasant wooded journey did not last for long. At Didmarton, where I bought provisions, we emerged on open and more populous roads. It was two o'clock when we left the village, and we began to look out for a lunching place. There was a grassy paddock on the left, which Spencer fancied ; but it belonged to a smart residential house with an elegantly laid-out garden, and I did not want to go there. Spencer called me a snob, but unmoved, I challenged him to ask himself. However, seeing a farm further down on the right, I went to the door and knocked. The house was shut up, and later we saw a notice on the gate saying that these premises were infected with swine fever. We tried the next farm. The boss was somewhere carting lime, and we had to find him before we could enter the field, a large, flat enclosure without water, shade, or shelter. The wind was cool, but the sun blazed down with almost summer heat ; the horses stood still under the only passable tree, whisking away the flies while we sat close to the hedge and ate, among other things, a quantity of tomatoes which were very refreshing.

From here we proceeded towards Tetbury, first by minor roads, and then by a main road, which was not as crowded as usual. This, however, made little difference to Jenny, who started the familiar programme of shying and saddle-slipping, with its equally familiar and tiresome sequel of entering the place on foot. We crossed a bridge, where people were standing about and talking, or leaning over the parapet to look for fish or think out some financial problem. The town had a familiar dead-alive look ; it was, of course, early closing day. This was a pity, for we had eaten all our provisions, and there would be nothing for breakfast. We were also badly in need of corn for the horses. We rode to the centre of the town, where I left Spencer with the ponies and went to call for letters. There was a registered packet for me containing some badly needed money, but I could not get it till the postmaster came back from his tea.

This would not be for half an hour, so I set myself to the problem of finding corn. Next to the post-office was an ironmonger's shop, at the door of which stood a woman with an intelligent eye. I asked her if she knew of a corn merchant whose store might be open on Thursday. She told me that the baker down the street was open and he kept poultry food and that sort of thing. So I left Spencer chatting with an admiring throng in the market-place, and wandered down to the baker's, where I bought a loaf for ourselves and a good supply of crushed oats for the horses. Meantime the postmaster had returned, and Spencer, having collected some useful information, loaded the corn in front of our saddles, and we clattered out of the town.

By the time we were clear of Tetbury it was getting late, and we decided to camp as soon as we found a suitable place. Leaving the main road, we turned right towards Cherington. A short distance down another lane we spied an encampment of gipsies, with a fire and tents and a horse and cart. They had found a stance and were busy with supper, the lucky devils ! But the elegance of our saddlery, in comparison with theirs, kindled a cheering glow of bourgeois satisfaction. And had I not five pounds in my pocket ? Though in a place with nothing to buy, one might as well have a sheaf of empty paper bags.

Twilight came, and still no house in sight. There must have been farms in plenty, but doubtless they were hidden in trees, with entrances upon some other road. For us, at least, they did not exist ; and we were beginning to feel chilly and forlorn, when we saw at the end of a lane a good-sized farm-house. We were about half a mile from Cherington village, where we could probably have found a pitch ; but this would be quieter, and was nearer anyhow, so we gave it a trial.

The house and garden had an almost monastic seclusion, being approached from the road by a narrow door in the blank forbidding face of a high stone wall. I opened the door and timidly walked up the flagged path. We had seen some foxhound puppies in the lane, which had encouraged Spencer ; the farmer must be keen on hunting, and therefore friendly. But as I passed a window, I had a glimpse of sweet peas in a cut-glass bowl. The sight of these flowers, so charmingly disposed, filled me with depression. One could not ask for tea here. Meanwhile the door had opened to my knock, and being confronted with the owner of the sweet peas, I explained my business. I asked for grazing, but not for tea.

We were shown a large field, or rather series of fields, for the dividing gates stood open, making the place like an immense suite of rooms in a hotel. It served as night pasture for a herd of Shorthorn cows, who stared at us with much interest, but made no closer investigation. However, we took the precaution of hanging the sack of oats out of their reach in a tree ; for a tent by itself is only an object of curiosity, while a tent with corn inside is well worth raiding.

Sadly we made our camp in the gathering dusk. The field faced the wrong way, and standing high, was exposed to the north wind, which felt more like March than mid-September. I suggested that we should walk to the village and prospect for tea, but Spencer said it was not worth while, and he would rather stay where he was. I offered to go myself and report, but this too was declined, and we made some kind of supper of dry bread, water, and broken fragments of corned beef. We lost no time in getting into our bags, for it was bitterly cold. I had some trouble with the air-mattress, for having lost the connecting tube of the little bellows, I had to blow up the wretched thing myself, and an air-mattress requires a surprising amount of wind to fill it.

Moreover, mine had developed a very slow puncture, the exact position of which we had been unable to discover : so that unless it was inflated to the utmost, it would by morning have sagged in the middle, leaving the sleeper's hip bone in contact with the hard cold ground. (And at Cherington the soil was shallow and baked with drought, so that tent-pegs were driven with difficulty, and several of the aluminium skewers got bent.) I puffed and blew with all my might, till my face was aflame and my temples bursting, and then rested a moment, pinching the valve to prevent the escape of all my precious breath. And after that, another spell of puffing, till the mattress was tight and rigid, and the air almost rushing back as I blew.

The days march had been good — indeed we were now always up to schedule, and our progress had developed the regularity of a railway time-table. But this was the worst camp we ever made. There was a sharp frost, and in spite of blanket and bag, I was too cold to sleep. Even *The Worst Journey* could offer no comfort, for if it is possible to sleep in a wet bag at − 50° F. why should I lie awake in a dry bag at +29° F. ? I heard the breath of cows and the munching of horses, for the air was very still ; and in the early morning, when the first grey glimmer of dawn crept over the frosty earth, there was a distant clatter of many hoofs on the road, as a string of hunters up from grass came out for exercise. As soon as there was enough light, I wriggled out of my bag and began to grope for my clothes. Dressing in a tent only 4 ft. 6 ins. at the apex is mostly a matter of crawling and stooping and swearing, and no one who has not tried it will realise the tediousness of putting on an awkward, many-buttoned garment like riding-breeches when one cannot stand upright. Presently the cowman came to the field and gathered the cows for milking. Our horses had disappeared, but later they were found at the furthest end of the furthest field, to which they had been attracted by the passing hunters.

The urgent problem was breakfast, and I confess that I did not feel very hopeful. There is nothing more foolish than to be in a land of plenty, with five pounds in your pocket, and yet unable to get food. However, I made up my mind to try the resources of Cherington ; and having packed my personal belongings, I left Spencer to strike camp and feed the horses, and hurried to the village by a field path I had noticed the previous evening. It was now about half-past seven, and the little place was just beginning to come to life. First I went to the post-office and asked if there were any place where we could get breakfast. The postmistress did not know, but perhaps they might oblige at the inn. This establishment, which was no proper inn, but a seedy-looking house with a licence to sell liquor for consumption off the premises, was not very helpful. An old woman, half asleep and strictly in morning dress, answered my knock, and said she had no time to be bothered with serving meals. Then I tried the shop, but of course it was not open. As I stood in the middle of the road, wondering where in the world I could raise some food and drink, I noticed a fat and kindly faced woman at a gate, seeing her husband off to work.

This set me thinking. Plump people are nearly always good-tempered, and if you have to ask a favour, choose someone with plenty of flesh on his bones, and you are more likely to get what you want. And again, this woman, having got rid of her husband for the day, would not be very busy, and might even welcome distraction and company. So I went up and told her all our troubles. She had tea to offer, and plenty of bread and butter, but there were no eggs or bacon in the house. However, if I liked to get something at the shop, which would soon be open, she would cook it for us. So I arranged for breakfast in half an hour, and dashed back for Spencer and the ponies.

(3) *Friday, Sept. 16 — Cherington to Farmington*

I returned to find the horses groomed and saddled, and we soon had the bags collected and Excalibur loaded for the march. I went down to the farmhouse to settle for the grazing, but they refused payment, and we set off in good heart, with the

cheering prospect of a cooked breakfast at a table.
While Spencer hitched up the horses in a neighbouring yard, I bought some bacon and tomatoes,
which were fried by our hostess, who had set the
table and had a fine fire blazing on the hearth. This
breakfast in a warm room, with a clean tablecloth
and the appetising fragrance and sizzle of frying bacon,
was among our most pleasant recollections. The
cottage was very old, with beautiful oak beams, but
we heard many complaints of its bad state of repair
and the difficulty of keeping it clean. The inhabitants
of picturesque cottages are all longing for concrete
bungalows with asbestos tiles, and in time, when all
the crumbling antiques have been transported to
America, they will have their hearts' desire. It is
a pity, but one cannot blame them, for from the
housewife's point of view an old house is awkward,
laborious, and often insanitary.

Leaving the village, we marched for a time across
the same high plateau land. But the wind had backed
to the south-west, and the temperature was rising by
leaps and bounds, which cheered our hearts and
gave the country a softer and more genial aspect.
Soon there were more trees, and we passed Lord
Bathurst's park, where a herd of deer was grazing.
Then we gradually climbed to another stretch of
plateau, following a deserted by-road in the direction
of Chedworth. The country was bleak and poor ; it
was mostly under the plough, with little livestock

anywhere. Hence there were few enclosed fields, and in many places the road was unfenced. Harebells were growing by the roadside, but the verges had nothing to offer but a scanty crop of harsh dry grass. Dwelling-houses were scattered and often invisible, and we would pass nothing but isolated groups of farm buildings, without a soul in sight. Many farmers were still busy with the harvest ; and the tawny stooks rose bright against the misty blue of the distant Wiltshire Downs, lending a note of colour to the empty quiet land.

The Cotswold country has a great reputation for beauty, which must largely depend on the charm of its houses and villages, for nature has not been lavish. A land with so little water, so few trees, and no hills worth mentioning — for though the Cotswolds are called " hills " they are really a succession of plateaux — has little natural grace, but the inhabitants have made up for these deficiencies by evolving a style of domestic architecture which has no equal in England, nor perhaps in the world. The soil is poor but it suits sheep, and in the days when sheep paid, and there was labour to fold them for the enrichment of corn land, Cotswold farmers were prosperous enough to build themselves the houses that are now so much admired and copied. In Britain, fine architecture is rarely found in the finest scenery, no doubt because great natural beauty is most often combined with material poverty. The Midlands and East Anglia are full

of magnificent churches and pretty villages, while
Scotland, which far excels them in landscape, has no
architecture to boast of, whether domestic or eccle-
siastical. The charm of Scotland, as of Wales and
Cumberland, depends on river, lake, and mountain ;
and "mountainy" men are poor, without the means,
even if they had the inclination, to build cathedrals
and manor-houses.

In this land without enclosures, lunch was a difficulty. There was no place where the horses could
be kept under control, and no grazing except on the
aftermath of unfenced hayfields, from which they
could stray on to other crops, or anywhere else they
pleased. At last we found a small paddock surrounded by high untrimmed hedges. There were
gaps in various places, and the grass was rough sour
bent and fog, but it was better than nothing, and we
turned in. While Spencer unsaddled, I picked a good
tinful of blackberries from the hedge, which was rich
in every kind of berry, hips and haws and bryony
and sloes. Our rest was much disturbed, for the
horses did not fancy the coarse herbage, and were
constantly trying to stray off through the gaps. We
took it in turns to herd them, the one eating, while
the other chased about the field.

After lunch we marched towards Chedworth,
where the eastern edge of the Cotswold plateau falls
sharply to the Vale of the White Horse. Here the
levels are broken by abrupt little valleys, with meagre

streams at the bottom, and we had a chance of watering the horses. From Chedworth, an attractive village, we marched towards Northleach. The land was richer here, with plenty of grass by the roadside and an abundant supply of blackberries. Trees were larger and more frequent, and with the trees came the mansions, which appear only in country which lends itself to park-making. We caught a glimpse of the wireless poles at Leafield — another landmark. There were plenty of pheasants about, and a hare or two. Travelling on horseback, one gets a good idea of road casualties among wild animals. I saw surprisingly few dead rabbits, but several weasels, and numberless flattened remains of hedgehogs. Poor little beasts, they move so slowly, what is their chance of escape ?

Near Northleach we emerged on a main road, but only to cross it, for there was a bridle-path that would take us into the town. Here we made enquiries, for we were not sure of the road to Farmington, near which we intended to camp that night. It was getting late, and the narrow winding streets were full of people who gazed at us with much interest. We saw some hikers heavily laden, which made us very conscious of the advantage of travelling with horses. As for our rucksacks, we had long since given up carrying them on our own backs — they were much too awkward and heavy. At Farmborough we had put them as they were in the white kit-bag and lashed it on to the pack.

We climbed out of Northleach by a by-road, looking for a farm, but none appeared. At last we saw a large house on the left. At the sound of hoofs the farmer's wife came out and gave us a welcome, but her husband was out with the binder about half a mile away, and would we ask him first. Spencer gave me the loan of Ladybird, and I rode off in search of the field indicated. In spite of her long march, the little mare was quite fresh, and we went off at a smart trot. The relief of riding a good horse at a good pace was enormous, and tired as I was, I quite enjoyed the trip. I saw the binder at the further end of a large field, and cantered down to it, threading my way among the stooks. It had broken down, and the farmer was lying under it. He said that this was the last acre of the last field, and the machine had worked perfectly till that moment. He had hoped to finish that evening, but now it was impossible. We could certainly have grazing, and he indicated a field near the house, with sheep in it.

We lost no time unpacking, as it was nearly dark. The field was level, but had been so heavily stocked with sheep that it was difficult to find a clean pitch, especially in the dim light. Tea had been promised, and we found an excellent meal ; but alas ! it was set in the parlour, where we were left to ourselves, without talk or company or local gossip. In the big prosperous Midland farms this was a common practice, and we missed the homely, cheerful surroundings of the West, where you always sat at the kitchen table and talked about stock and crops and changing times. The farm was large and more fully mechanised than any we had so far seen. Much corn was grown, and there was a good stock of sheep. We were able to buy a supply of oats for the horses, for which I was thankful, as the grazing of the past two days had been of medium quality.

That night was fine and much milder than the previous one. The lights of aeroplanes were moving among the stars, and for some hours they droned without ceasing. The tent was alive with daddies, and though I killed a dozen or so before settling down to read, I was forced to break off at frequent intervals and catch a few more. My tent was of a terra-cotta colour, while Spencer's was white, and we noticed that mine, when lighted up, attracted twice the number of insects. Most of them, however, entered the space between the fly-sheet and the tent itself, and in the morning the apex of the fly-sheet would be crowded with moths, earwigs, and daddies — especially the last.

(4) *Saturday, Sept. 17, to Monday, Sept. 19*
Oddington Interlude

Our next stage — Farmington to Oddington — was a short ten miles. Properly speaking we should have advanced to some point north of Moreton-in-Marsh, but my friend V. R. had invited us to spend the week-end in an empty house at Oddington, and this was our last chance of pitching the week-end camp near some acquaintance. Also we met our respective parents there, and exchanged news and received letters.

This march was uneventful and quite pleasant. The country was more fertile and well-wooded. At Bourton-on-the-Water we bought food, and wired to Oddington, for at our present rate of progress we should arrive before we were expected. The horses splashed gaily through the ford, and we admired the quaint little bridges that give the village its unusual charm.

As we rode we discussed plans. The thought of riding Jenny to the Border was a dismal one, and I was seriously considering the purchase of a trap or float, if one could be obtained locally, in which Excalibur could pull the pack instead of carrying it. I would drive, and Spencer could continue riding Ladybird, while the wretched Jenny must be sold. She was a nice-looking mare and in foal, so that it should not be hard to find a buyer. This plan would save time on the march, as it would be much quicker to harness Excalibur and throw the bags into a trap than to load him with the pack-saddle. Also there would be one less horse to catch, groom, and feed ; and we might be able to trot a little, and thus without increasing the daily mileage, shorten and vary the actual hours spent on the road. As we talked, Jenny pointed the moral by shying violently at an enormous cream-coloured horse-box. There were plenty of hunters about, and in one field we noticed a portable milking bail — the first I had seen in actual use.

We reached Oddington, and rode through it without seeing anyone we knew. The empty house was on a hill above the village, and I suggested that we should leave the horses and baggage there before introducing ourselves to V. R., whose large and important-looking new home dominated the place from the other side. We hitched up the horses at the gate, unpacked, and dumped the kit in the porch. We were just thinking of turning the horses loose in the orchard and having lunch, when the farmer next door, with whom V. R. had arranged for the grazing of our ponies, appeared at the gate. Collecting the horses, we followed him to a field across the road, and then returned and ate our lunch on the lawn.

The house had some furniture left in it ; we slept in beds, and had meals at a table. The kitchen range was lighted, so that we revelled in glorious baths ; and on Sunday, while Spencer overhauled and cleaned the saddlery, I did some mending and washing of clothes. In the evening there was much telling of adventures, such as they were, and discussing of plans for the future. We looked at maps and measured distances, and decided that if we could reach Hartington by the following Saturday night, we would spend the week-end at a hotel, as the supply of friends on the route was now exhausted.

On Sunday morning we saw the farmer, Mr. X, driving out in a neat little trap drawn by a smart pony. Spencer thought he might sell it ; and although I was not hopeful, it seemed worth while to visit him, and ask if he knew anyone who had a trap or float for sale. He agreed that a trap would suit us much better than a pack-horse, and rang up a man in Stow who might be useful, but without result. The trouble was that most of the local farmers had given up their traps so long ago that they were either sold or unfit for the roads. Later on, in Yorkshire, when Spencer was gone and the pack-horse scrapped, I saw plenty of suitable vehicles, but at this critical moment the thing we wanted seemed unprocurable.

Later, when I was buying eggs at another farm, I noticed a float standing in the cart-shed. It was clumsily built and unnecessarily heavy, but was otherwise suitable, and hearing that the owner was leaving at Michaelmas, I offered to buy it. But she refused to sell anything before the sale, which would not be held for another ten days. We could not afford to wait, so this idea, like many another, had to be scrapped.

We had a magnificent Sunday dinner with V. R. Sitting at her polished table in our way-worn breeches, with enormous appetites and unfeigned delight in good food and drink, we must have seemed rather crude and out of place, but this did not spoil our enjoyment. Spencer and V. R. soon discovered a common passion for hunting, and were talking sixteen to the dozen.

Later, as we sat in the drawing-room, the sky became very dark, and without the slightest warning came a brilliant flash of lightning and crack of thunder overhead. Then the heavens opened, and the deluge that followed would have washed us out of our tents had we been in them. We had been invited to tea with the Editor of *The Countryman* at Idbury Manor, which was not more than five miles away, and were planning to go on horseback. But it was still raining in torrents, and borrowing an umbrella from V. R., we pelted down to the village inn and bespoke a car. This caused disappointment at Idbury, where the whole cavalcade was expected, but to be quite truthful, we rather enjoyed a rest from the saddle. The tea was delicious, and we had a long talk about past adventures, future plans, and all kinds of other things. We were shown the editorial offices, with views from the windows that would make even office work seem desirable, and the garden and swimming-pool, and a fruit-bottling plant and an Aga cooker : and having seen all this, we were quite sure that the producers of *The Countryman* have as good a time as the readers. And we met Sylvia Townsend Warner, who was not at all like her books. This always happens with authors, and Miss Warner is lucky in being only different from, and not worse than the imaginary portrait painted by the reader. Authors, or indeed any kind of artist, should be met before their works are tackled, and then there is some chance of knowing them as they are, apart from illusions created by their work. Or should they not be met at all ? For perhaps their work is the true self, and the personal presence a ghost. I don't know : anyhow Miss Warner was very charming in the flesh, and I hope she found me the same.

We returned to supper by the kitchen fire, and then enjoyed our last night on a bed, which was the more delightful as the thunderstorm had left the country streaming with water. It was good to snuggle down in blankets and read *The Worst Journey* by an electric reading-lamp. Most of us never get the maximum of enjoyment out of the common amenities of civilised life, because we are never forced to do without them, and cannot even imagine what life would be like in their absence. To be really appreciated, they must be welcomed like long-lost friends, whom we did not expect to see again. No fatted calf, however fat, will ever seem as good as that which is set before a prodigal son.

VII

Warwickshire

(1) *Monday, Sept. 19 — Oddington*
to Willington

ON Monday morning we decided to make a last effort
to procure a trap, for if we could get one locally, it
would be easy to leave Jenny with Mr. X, for disposal
at the forthcoming Michaelmas sale. Leaving Excalibur in the field, we saddled Ladybird and Jenny,
and trotted up to Stow-on-the-Wold, where we had
heard of one or two people who might know of possible
vehicles. It was all very vague, but just worth trying.
The ride was pleasant, for unhampered by the pack-
horse, we could go at a good pace. But our enquiries
were unavailing. There appeared to be no trap or
float of any description in Stow. We were given
the name of a man at Moreton-in-Marsh who might
know of something, but that was all. We might, of
course, see what we wanted in a cart-shed by the
roadside, as we had done at Farmborough, or we
might find one at a Michaelmas sale, for which the
season was approaching. So we decided to carry on
as we were, and keep our eyes open for developments.

The chief objection to the present arrangement was the awkwardness of Jenny. The pack-saddle was working quite well, and in summer, when longer daylight would have enabled us to have tea before tackling any camp work, its disadvantages would not have been so marked. I could, of course, have bought another riding horse ; but it is very difficult to get anything suitable at a moment's notice, especially when you are not prepared to pay a fancy price.

We returned to Oddington, lunched off the remains of our week-end stores, gathered our kit and packed. We rode through the village past V. R.'s new house, where we stopped to say good-bye and have our photographs taken. Crossing the Oxford-Worcester line at Addlestrop we marched north, leaving Moreton-in-Marsh on the left. It hardly seemed worth while to make a special excursion to look for something which probably did not exist. The day was cloudy, with a south-west wind, and although there was no rain, the sky had a wild unsettled look, with toppling masses of cumulus cloud on the horizon.

We plodded on through park-like undulating country with trees and prosperous-looking farms. We were off the Cotswold plateau, and for many miles to come should be travelling through a land which is considered typically English : though as the scenery of England is most amazingly diversified, I cannot see why any one district should appear more

typical than any other. Before long we passed the
Four Counties Stone, where Oxfordshire, Glouces-
tershire, Worcestershire, and Warwickshire meet.
Much felling of trees and carting of wood was in
progress, and we passed lorries laden with logs, at
which the horses shied. The left-hand signposts
showed Stratford-on-Avon, and the right-hand ones
Banbury ; only once did I see " Oxford 26 miles ".
I was glad that our route would not take us much
nearer. I had been there last May in the Summer
Term, when everything was looking at its best ; yet
I vowed that nothing would ever induce me to return.
It was like meeting an old friend after many years,
and finding him altered beyond recognition ; only in
this case the friend had not aged but grown strangely
and horribly new. Worst of all were the roads and
the frightful traffic ; in the midst of that, where can
one find a place for that quiet meditation which is the
soul of scholarship ? However, there is no sense in
grumbling, for Oxford must keep up to date or die,
and if this is what the young people want, let them
have it, and good luck to them. Only don't ask the
old fogies to come up and admire. They have crept
into the shadows, along with the last hansom and the
ultimate horse-tram. Let them moulder in peace,
for if you haul them blinking into the light of your
new day, they may spit venomously, like bad-tempered
cockroaches. Once I had thought of spending my old
age in Oxford ; but now it will be on some forgotten

headland of the West, where there are hills and seas and clouds and the road is too rough for anything but a pony, that I shall end my days if I get the chance.

We marched north quietly and steadily. The afternoon wore on, and I rode in a dream, as if hypnotised by the level road and brooding trees and quiet cloudy sky. There was no sun, but the light in the west was perceptible, and as we travelled north, it always fell on my left cheek. This was the first time I was definitely aware of it, but each succeeding day at the same time I looked for the light on the left, and thought, we are always moving north, and sooner or later shall be in Scotland.

The architecture was beginning to change. Stone houses of the Cotswold type were giving way to the brick and timbered variety, and towers were being replaced by spires, either by themselves, or as an addition to a squat tower. There was less land under the plough, and the startling white faces of Hereford cattle peered over well-trimmed thorn hedges. But trees were the dominant note — trees with long roots and spreading branches, elms for the most part, showing a deep and fertile soil. In ancient times this Midland country must have been an almost impenetrable forest ; what labour must have gone to clearing it ! The foliage was still green and heavy, and I should like to have seen the place in winter, with the tracery of bare branches furred with rime and glistening in the pale sunlight. Trees, like women, are charming as individuals, but terrifying in the mass. Nothing is more beautiful than the details of a tree, from the harsh wrinkled bark to the almost invisible network of veins in a young leaf, and nothing more intriguing than the history of its slow and secret growth. But serried trees are like armies converging upon you, devouring the daylight, precluding escape. To live in a great forest, however beautiful, would be a slow madness, driving one at last to the mountains above or the sea beyond — to any refuge with space and a far horizon.

Towards evening we found ourselves near Willington, having logged ten miles since three o'clock. There were plenty of farms about, and we tried a small attractive-looking place near the road. The owner told us he would have been very glad to oblige us, but he kept a stallion, and could not take any strange mares. He suggested that we should try his brother's farm, which was about 200 yards farther on. We took his advice. This was a larger place, very neat, with a timbered house full of old beams and an immense porch like a church. I went up the flagged path and knocked. The door was opened by a young woman with a baby in her arms. As usual we were referred to the master of the house, who was busy in the yard. Returning, I found him already deep in conversation with Spencer, and we were taken to a small paddock of about half an acre, in which there were three sheep. This was our smallest camping ground, as the field at Kingston had been our largest. Being next to the road it was rather public, and our camp work was watched through gaps in the hedge by a crowd of small children. But the grass was good and the horses showed no inclination to break out.

We returned to the house. The baby had been put to bed, and we found tea laid in an elegant parlour, which was more like a drawing-room. There were the usual boiled eggs, and piles of cakes, both home-made and " bought ". The farmer's wife sat and talked to us while we ate, and later her husband joined us, and we had a long conversation. Even here Spencer knew the names of some local hunting celebrities. Cubbing had begun, and in the early hours of the morning we heard the ring of horses' hoofs on the hard road.

We asked our host if he knew of a trap or a float. He said that he had one himself, and would show it us in the morning. It had been laid up for several years, and we reflected that it would probably be too dilapidated to stand a long journey. After breakfast we made an inspection. The trap had once been good, but it was spoilt with disuse, and almost smothered with the junk that always accumulates in laid-up vehicles. Cleared and cleaned, it would look very different, but one glance at the shafts told us that it was too small for either of our horses. There was nothing for it but to go on as we were.

I confess that at this point, when we had accom-

plished nearly half the journey to the Border, I began
to feel rather despondent. It would be awful to ride
Jenny all day for another fortnight, especially through
the North Midlands, where the traffic would be much
worse than it had been hitherto. We had overcome
all the initial difficulties, and had reached that rather
boring stage of any enterprise, when you have sur-
mounted the obstacles and are merely plodding on
and on. The country was not very interesting, and
our daily marches, regular as clockwork, seemed to
yield nothing exciting, nor even mildly entertaining.
This, no doubt, was one of those flat uninspired
intervals, a dull connecting thread, like the tedious
passages with which epic poets are forced to link their
heroic episodes. Such things are unavoidable, and
no one can grumble if the longueurs of the Trojan
War or the Loss of Paradise are repeated on a pony
trek in England. Though our purple patches, alas !
were less purple than they might have been.

By one of those flashes of intuition that illuminate
without helping, I was aware that my patient and un-
complaining comrade was completely fed up with his
job ; and I do not blame him. It takes some imagina-
tion to see that a long ride on horseback, which sounds
so thrilling in prospect, may in actual fact be immensely wearisome and monotonous, especially with
a pack-horse, and a companion who does not think
or act as you do. That is, unless you are a born
traveller who can shake down anywhere and with

anyone, and these unluckily are rare. So as I lay in my tent at Willington, I pondered deeply on this problem. Two women left alone will often fight like cats over trifles, while a man and a woman travelling together will end (so they say) in love or hate. The first being unthinkable, must it be the last ? We'll hope not. On this I fell asleep.

(2) *Tuesday, Sept. 20 — Willington to Bishop's Tachbrook*

We woke to a dull morning with fine drizzling rain. To strike camp in the wet is always a miserable business, for everything must be packed inside the tents, and the horse be loaded at top speed. But the rain soon ceased, and we continued our journey through typical Warwickshire scenery. At Honington we stopped to buy food. This was a charming village, with old cottages round a green, and a big house with posts and chains. A lorry loaded with straw caused some commotion among the horses, but otherwise our progress was steady and uneventful. At lunch-time we saw a triangular paddock, bounded on two sides by muddy water, and on the third by a railway embankment. We entered from the road through a gap in the hedge, and turning the horses loose, sat near the gap to eat. But the ponies were restless, looking for a drink, and the ditches that enclosed the field were sunk too deep for them to reach, and we had to take them outside and water them one by one at a sluggish stream. Presently a train passed, causing them all to stampede ; but after this excitement they settled down and we finished our meal in peace. While loading, we heard a noise like an approaching train, and were careful to loosen the halters from the railings to which they were fastened ; but it proved to be a passing car, and all was well.

Presently we emerged on the main road to Warwick, which lay on our route about twelve miles further north. We should, of course, have reached the town more quickly by taking the major road, but in a short time we turned right, and found ourselves on a long deserted stretch of the Foss Way. The construction of a modern thoroughfare on the Roman foundation gives a curious impression, for the centres of population have changed, and this road, so straight and well-kept, leads nowhere in particular, and is almost empty of traffic. It was uncanny to see its vacant length, like a strip of grey-black ciré ribbon, drawn taut and vanishing in perspective over a distant rise. We travelled three or four miles without meeting anything but a man on a cycle. Big trees bordered the road, and squirrels would often cross our path and dart with incredible speed from the ground to the upper branches. The agility and grace of these little beasts is amazing ; if we had a fraction of it we should be happy for life.

Warwickshire

At intervals the Foss Way was crossed by busy roads with a roar of traffic, mostly commercial. Having avoided the main routes north, we had to cross rather than follow the major roads, which was very fortunate, for the traffic in North Warwickshire and South Derbyshire was worse than anywhere else on the journey. The aeroplanes, thank God, were gone, but we could hear the continuous buzz of motors, although we rarely met one. Tractors were much in evidence, mostly employed in cultivating stubbles or in autumn ploughing, and their hum and clatter added to the noise of a mechanised countryside.

Presently, as we topped a rise, we saw below us a large traction engine, which with some difficulty was manœuvring into a gate. A sale had been held in the field, which was strewn with implements and miscellaneous junk awaiting removal. These things, useful and even smart in their natural place, had, when jumbled fortuitously together, a look of abandonment and betrayal that cried upon my pity, so much did they remind me of my own chattels in the field at Newton. As we drew level, they were hitching the traction engine to an immense corn-drill. Clouds of steam drifted across the road, and I rode with caution, as Jenny had a marked distaste for steam, which was white and connected in her mind with trains. I wondered how long it would take the engine and its uncouth load to clear the gateway ; and then which way would it turn, and last, if it turned in our direction, would it travel quickly enough to overtake us? Very unlikely, especially if we put on a little speed. I urged Jenny forward, which roused protests from Spencer ; why tire the horses by excessive speeding? I had not the moral courage to confess that I wished to avoid the engine. We never saw it again, and I fancy it must have turned the other way.

There was an increasing number of Hereford cattle, and also Clun sheep from Shropshire. I saw two sights that were new to me — a herd of Blue Albion cows, and a field of maize. Later, we had a distant view of factory chimneys — our first glimpse of the industrial Midlands.

We skirted the village of Bishop's Tachbrook, and turned towards Warwick. We had made very good progress, and could have reached the town that night ; but having already marched twenty miles, we decided to look for a pitch. It was a fine evening, and we ambled peacefully along, scanning the country-side, which at this point was largely devoted to dairy farming and market gardening. On the left was a sewage farm, from which unappetising odours drifted on the breeze. We kept to windward of this nuisance, and at last spied a large farm at the end of a longish avenue. Leaving Spencer at the gate, I turned Jenny towards the house. She crabbed un-willingly along the drive, neighing to her lost com-panions. What sense was there in starting a solo journey at this time of night ? I always pitied the horses for their ignorance : they never knew where they would be taken, or whether we planned to keep them trekking for the rest of their natural lives. Though I suppose that by this time they had come to associate the setting sun with journey's end and food and grazing. They certainly connected these things with side tracks and farm entrances, for, left to themselves, they would always turn right or left sooner than go straight ahead. And they still wished to turn south, little knowing that they were many weary miles from Cornwall.

I had hardly reached the house when the farmer's wife came out. It was a superior place and I felt a little nervous. When I asked for grazing she looked rather distant and doubtful, taking us no doubt for hikers of some kind, and then said, well, they didn't usually do that kind of thing, but she would ask her husband. I proceeded to explain that we were not hikers but farmers on tour, who were riding through England to study comparative methods of farming. This, if not strictly true, was near enough, and she began to look interested. I asked if they took the *Farmers' Weekly*, and hearing that they did, enquired if she had seen my articles on Bodmin Moor. She had, and after that she made me very welcome. I signalled to Spencer, who was waiting at the gate with Ladybird and Excalibur ; and then the farmer, who had joined his wife outside the house, took us to a large level field, not quite as big as the one at Kingston, but equally exposed, and full of sheep. There was no lee hedge, the only shelter being a wood-pile, where the ground was too muddy for camping ; but as it was a good night we made the best of a pitch in the open.

This was my favourite time of day. The march, with whatever it held of monotony and discomfort, was over. Spencer could console himself with innumerable cigarettes ; but I am no smoker, and riding in the rear, I had little to do but watch the gentle swaying of Excalibur's pack, on which the words " Finest Fish Meal " acted as a kind of hypnotic charm. Over, too, was the distasteful business of accosting strangers, and asking them the favour of grazing, and, worse still, of tea. Although we had never been refused (for at Cherington we had not even asked) I was always pursued by the foolish dread of rebuff. But when all the business of seeking and asking was accomplished, and we were safe in a field with the prospect of tea first, and then a talk, and after that a few minutes with Cherry-Garrard, I was well content. Evening was always best, and each setting sun, as it fell on my left cheek, was bringing us nearer to Scotland.

Tea was set in the large dining-room. The house was brick-built and slated, solid, square, and fairly modern. The outbuildings were spacious and up to date, and the large herd of cows was milked by machinery. One of the daughters was working on the farm ; we had seen her helping her father to dress sheep. After tea the farmer came in and talked for a time. There were the usual complaints about labour — the impossibility of trade-union hours for stockmen, and the difficulty of getting reliable cow-men. Sheep prices were deplored, and the alarming increase of maggot trouble, especially among flocks on rich land. On many farms in late summer and autumn the dressing of affected sheep is a daily task ; and they could hardly believe their ears when I told them that my Cheviot flock on the moor had kept free of the pest for the whole year.

We enquired for a trap, but without much hope, and quite without success. They told us that in this district such things had long since disappeared. Neither were there any farm sales due in the next few days. So we abandoned the idea, and returning to the tents, we held a council of war.

Putting Jenny aside, the main difficulty was corn. For the last two days we had been unable to get any, and it looked as if we must be prepared to carry a supply with us. The load on the pack-horse was heavy and bulky enough without any addition, and it was impossible to carry more than two days' supply on the riding horses. Every day as the season ad-vanced and we travelled further north, the grass would become scantier and its feeding value less. Before long we should be in mountain districts with rough sour herbage. The horses must have corn somehow. There were several options. We could buy a second pack-horse, but this meant more expense and an extra mouth to feed. We could scrap the pack and carry on with the two riding horses, but that involved scrapping the tents as well, and finding night quarters for two people, a difficult and costly matter. Or I might carry on alone, riding one horse and leading the other with my equipment and the corn. Or I might scrap the camping gear and continue the journey alone with one pony.

The last course was the one chosen. I was sorry to abandon the camping equipment, as a tent makes for economy and independence. A field which must in any case be got for your horse is easier to find than a bed, and costs far less. But I did not much fancy the business of leading a pack-horse on crowded roads, and still less of having to cope single-handed with packing, camp work, and the feeding and grooming of two horses. I asked Spencer whether, if he had no special use for Ladybird, he would sell her to me, which he agreed to do. After some discussion, we arranged to proceed to Hartington as we were. We would spend the week-end there, and then separate. The camping gear and pack-saddle could be sent on to Scotland and Jenny and Excalibur sold at a local farm sale or market.

This plan had much to commend it. I should have a companion for the next few days, which would be the worst as far as traffic was concerned. After Hartington I hoped, apart from the narrow corridor between Rochdale and Huddersfield, to follow the Pennine range by unfrequented roads. I should have a good horse, and unencumbered by baggage (for my few personal possessions could be carried in one of the rucksacks) I could make fair progress. Apart from this, the war scare was developing with alarming rapidity, and at any moment Spencer might be called up. It was better for him to be somewhere more accessible, and for myself to be independent.

Many people have since asked me what I would have done had war broken out. Being now without home or job, and with practically no relations, I should have carried on. Another fortnight would see me to the end of my journey, and there would be plenty of time then to look for other work. I have lived too long in the level-headed, slow-moving farming community to be easily stampeded. Those who say the war is inevitable are not only public enemies, but liars. Nothing is inevitable but the slow processes of Nature. We cannot avoid death, but we can avoid war, and those who say we can't should be shot as traitors to civilisation.

This discussion lasted a long time, and as it was carried on in the dark outside our tents, we were very cold before it was done. As I snuggled down in my bag and tried to warm my icy feet (for the old-maidish hot-water bottle had been scrapped at Glastonbury), I had a sense of great relief that all these problems were settled. I did not much look forward to the lone trail, but for a solitary woman nervousness is a luxury that cannot be afforded, and solo travelling has many compensations. You have no one to consider but yourself ; you can go where and when you like, stop when you want to, eat what and when you fancy, without reference to the curious and unpredictable tastes of a comrade. You are not really alone, for you have your horse, and everyone is kind to a lone traveller. You get more talk, more friendliness, more hospitality : you see far more of the country. This I expected, and my hopes were confirmed by actual experience.

(3) *Wednesday, Sept. 21 — Bishop's Tachbrook to Maxstoke*

The morning was dull, but later the sun came out, and the south-west wind was mild and fresh. We left the farm with the good wishes of all, and were soon on the main road to Warwick. This was a nasty stretch. The normal rush of traffic was increased by numerous farmers' cars and livestock lorries, for it was market day. I dismounted, and walked the remaining two miles into the town. Warwick, with Glossop, was the largest town we entered. We might have given it a miss, had we not wanted to buy corn and one or two Ordnance sheets. We crossed the bridge, from which you get that striking view of the Castle beyond the river. I saw it out of the tail of my eye, but could not stop to look, for a bridge swarming with traffic is the last place to halt with horses.

We skidded down the other side and marched into the town. At the entrance to the Castle stood a custodian, watching the riot of cars with serene detachment. Breaking his meditation, we asked for a corn merchant. We were standing at a place where several roads converged, a provincial Piccadilly Circus. Pointing across this vortex, he showed us a one-way street. " Half way down there, on the left ! " he yelled, and then went back to his dreams. No one would want to be shown the Castle to-day.

We hauled the horses across, and crept down the one-way street in single file, for we were entering it from the wrong end. There was a very quiet yard at the miller's, into which we fled with relief, leaving the traffic to roar past like waves outside a breakwater. We bought a good supply of crushed oats, and persuaded them to let us leave the horses there while we did the rest of our shopping. War-wick is a charming old town, and I was sorry to have no leisure to explore it. But if we were to reach Hartington on Saturday, we must push on, for our schedule allowed no margin for possible accidents and delay. We found the necessary maps, bought some choice provisions, and left the town in the direction of Kenilworth. This road was a nightmare, and the B road on which we travelled later was not much

better. In this part of the country there is so much
motor transport that the major thoroughfares will not
take it all, and it spills over on to anything with a
possible surface that leads anywhere. We met a great
many livestock lorries, which caused much shying and
swerving, though Jenny was not fresh enough for her
best performances.

Not far from Kenilworth we were stopped by a
man who looked like a farmer. He asked if we were
going for a riding tour, and we told him of our plans.
He then enquired if we had heard of two girls who
had given a modern version of Dick Turpin's ride to
York, and went on to say that he was interested in
the riding-school from which they had hired their
horses. It seemed that they had ridden seventy miles
a day, but for two days only, and when he seemed
rather contemptuous of our pace, we explained that
we were not out for speed, and had already been a
fortnight on the road, and should need as much again
to take us to Scotland. After some further talk we
left him, and before long reached the outskirts of
Kenilworth.

This is a disappointing place. I had expected an
old-fashioned country town and found instead a long
raw street, in which every second building seemed
to be a garage or a cinema. We plodded drearily
along, threading our way between stationary cars
and moving traffic, with everyone staring at the un-
wonted spectacle. We stopped at the post-office,

where Spencer expected letters, and a pair of new breeches ; the ones he was wearing were getting beyond repair. While I was minding the horses outside, a crowd of children collected, and stared with amusement at poor patient Excalibur. " It's a camel, that's what it is ! " said one. " No 't'aint," was the snubbing reply, " it's only a horse."

At the end of this long and ugly street we turned left, and passed the Castle. Here were a few pleasant old houses, and a custodian in uniform, like the one at Warwick. But a car was drawn up at the entrance, from which sightseers were emerging, so that he had to pull himself together and attend to his job. A little further on I saw the word " FORD " painted in white on a wall. I could not imagine what it referred to, and with so much traffic about, it is not surprising that my mind ran on Ford cars, and missed the simple and primitive meaning of the word. But there was a ford, and we soon came to it. The stream was only a few inches deep, but cars splashed noisily through, with fans of water spouting from their wheels. The horses had a good drink, and Jenny forgot to shy.

Two or three miles further on, in the heart of the country, we saw our first specimen of ribbon development. There was a row of semi-detached houses, perhaps half a mile in length, each with a garage and a garden, and the usual supply of baby Austins, perambulators, small dogs, lawn-mowers, and modernistic curtains. I wondered vaguely where the inhabitants went to work. Perhaps at Kenilworth, but in that case they must all be garage proprietors or cinema managers. Or at Coventry, which was not far away. Or were they all retired ? The country was everywhere amazingly tidy. Hedges were trimmed, gates in good order and properly hung, and everyone's garden like a new pin. Some people, not contented with their own lawns, had even troubled to mow the grass verge of the public road.

Later we had a distant view of Coventry, which lay about five miles to the north-east. Seen from afar and veiled in smoke, the slender tapering chimneys had a grace of their own, and made a not unworthy background for the beautiful spire of the parish church.

It was time for lunch. A little further on we noticed some men hedging, and close to the place where they worked was a delightful little paddock of about two acres, with lush grass and plenty of shade. We asked leave to halt, and they unfastened a permanently wired gate to let us in. Here we had the finest mid-day rest we had ever enjoyed, and after our tedious morning's march it was all the more welcome, especially when we had excellent provisions from Warwick to eat ourselves, and a liberal feed for the horses.

We saddled up with reluctance, and went on our way. There was a lot of heavy transport on the road, but the horses were getting accustomed to it, and gave little trouble. Presently we heard an uproar ahead, and came to the place, near Meriden, where our route intersected the Birmingham-Coventry main road. At that moment it was impossible to cross, and we stood watching the torrent. Cars, motor cycles, buses, vans of all shapes and sizes and colours, removal pantechnicons, and enormous lorries loaded with timber or rails or machinery, streamed past at great speed, for the road was straight and wide. At last a lull came, and seizing the opportunity we dashed across. We were now travelling on by-ways towards Maxstoke, but the noise of this and other main roads pursued us like the roaring of surf. We began to climb, and presently emerged on a ridge which runs parallel to the high ground at Coleshill. To the north-west lay a flattish stretch of country, dominated by the chimneys of a large power station, and beyond that, about twelve miles away, was Birmingham.

We passed through Maxstoke, a quiet village with a ruined priory which now forms part of a farm. The arch of the old gateway serves as entrance to the yard, and as we rode by, a couple of cart-horses came out of it. The sun was near setting, and we began to look for a place to camp. Just outside the village we spied a nice-looking farm. I went up to the house and knocked. The door was opened, but not very wide, by an elderly woman, who eyed me suspiciously. With a disarming smile I explained our business and asked for grazing. But none was forthcoming. Her husband was away for the night, and she would do nothing without him. Could she suggest another place near by, as it was getting late ? She mentioned a small-holding half a mile away, and rather despondently we trekked in that direction. This was our first refusal, and it discouraged me. We were near to towns — too near — and in such places people are much less friendly. However, I noticed with satisfaction that every other cottage displayed a notice of " Teas ", and even if we could not get a pitch, we need not starve. Maxstoke is well within the radius of Birmingham cycling clubs, and in summer nearly every inhabitant is ready to cater for their needs.

The small-holding turned out to be a long low cottage with a collection of newish, ramshackle, galvanised outhouses, strongly reminiscent of an Australian homestead. Outside were the usual notices about Teas and Minerals, with the addition of Camping Sites. The grazing was doubtful, as the small fields looked very bare ; but they thought it could be managed, and the horses were turned loose in a paddock with a couple of large white sows. We were advised not to camp ourselves in this field, as the sows were mischievous, but we should find the next one, in which two tents were already erected, quite comfortable. So we threw the baggage over the hedge and followed it ourselves. This field, which was about three acres, was used in winter for football and in summer for camping. There were goal-posts in the middle, and round the hedge, neatly disposed at regular intervals, were a number of dust-bins for campers' rubbish. We pitched our tents at the furthest corner from the other ones, and then discovered that they belonged to a week-end party, and were now deserted.

We went to the house and ordered tea. The family were at their own meal, and we were escorted to the tea-room, a wooden shack in the rear, fitted with benches and an iron stove, rough tables, and a kind of verandah in front. It was very draughty and dusty, and a shower pattered dismally on the iron roof. Presently tea was brought, and we fell to, but without our usual gusto. Suddenly we heard a clamour outside, and a band of youths burst in, in the strange miscellaneous clothes affected by members of cycling clubs. Most were in shorts, but some had plus-fours in large patterns, and wore brightly coloured sports shirts. Their cycles were racing models, immensely smart and well-kept, and they were busily hauling them out of the rain and stacking them on the verandah. They gazed at us with surprise, and then retired to an inner room, where they had an uproarious meal. They were members of a Birmingham cycling club, who met after work hours, rode out to some place in the country, had a meal, and went home again. They are fine institutions, and we were to see a good deal more of them in the North.

We finished our tea and went back to the tents. The rain had ceased, but a strong wind was roaring in the trees, and the distant hum of traffic was plainly heard in the lulls. The clouds were lit up by a glare reflected from towns and factories.

It was good to have detailed maps again, and Spencer was busy working out a route for to-morrow. One more day of semi-industrial country, and then we should cross the Trent, and apart from the Rochdale-Huddersfield corridor, would see no more horrors. The march from Tachbrook to Maxstoke was the least pleasant of all, except perhaps that from Holmbridge to Cragg Vale, of which more in its place.

Next morning we got some further idea of our quarters. Besides the tea-room there was a range of lavatories, and a shanty where you could get a penny wash and brush-up. In the house chocolate and cigarettes were on sale. The farmyard was full of notices forbidding you to enter the buildings or touch the stock. The owner of the place was primarily a coal merchant, but combined with this business the rearing of pigs, calves, and poultry, as well as catering for campers. A strenuous, but no doubt a profitable life. Our bill was a little higher than usual, as we had to pay for camping as well as grazing ; but the food was cheap, as it continued to be throughout the North, apart from places devoted to the wealthier type of visitor. The North, as everyone knows, is much more democratic than the South, and this difference is reflected in all the details of life and travel. To people moving slowly like ourselves, it was amusing to watch the gradual, almost imperceptible shift of custom and outlook. Day by day there seemed little change, and yet what a world between Badminton and Haworth !

(4) *Thursday, Sept. 22 — Maxstoke to Clifton*

By morning the wind had dropped, and the cloudy sky showed signs of breaking. We packed, threw the baggage over the hedge, and saddled the horses. We rode first in an easterly direction, and then turned north along a ridge, keeping on high ground all the time. There was a wide view to the west and north-west, in which the tall spire of Coleshill church made a striking and graceful landmark. The power-station, though it stood low and in the most rustic surroundings, was even more dominant. It had three or four chimneys and a number of bulging, boiler-like objects from which steam was ascending. When we started, it appeared to be about two miles away in the north-west ; then we slowly drew level, and finally about noon, we saw the last of it in the far south-west. Never was any man-made landmark more persistent.

We rode through narrow, leafy lanes, with

cottages here and there, which invariably offered Teas and Minerals. In the distance chimneys would appear singly or in small clusters, sprouting suddenly from fields like mushrooms. The isolated rural collieries were even more surprising. In the midst of quiet fields, where cows were grazing, or plough-teams dawdling to and fro, you would see a demure slag-heap, and black pit-head buildings, with a wheel rotating busily but quite unobtrusively, like an antique spinning-wheel converted to modern use. Not far off would be a row of miners' cottages, all in one block in the proper urban tradition, as if the countryside were not wide enough to let them spread.

For the last few days I had been in the habit of carrying our food in a small knapsack on my back. I had bought enough in Warwick to last for two days, and in consequence the bag was fairly heavy. At midday, when we were thinking of finding a place for lunch, I missed it. We had made two wayside halts that morning, and I must have left it at one place or the other, for on these occasions I always took it off to rest myself. Leaving Spencer, I trotted back to the last halt. My switch was there, but no knapsack. The first halt was two or three miles further back, and as there was a good chance that the bag, or at any rate its contents, had already been picked up, I decided not to waste precious time and energy in looking further. There was a spare tin of tongue in one of the kit-bags, and we could raise some bread and butter at a cottage. Jenny was wild to rejoin her companions, and as the saddle took a fit of slipping, I had some difficulty in mounting and heartily wished that I had not bothered to pick up the switch, which was a hedge specimen, and of no earthly value. I cantered back and rejoined Spencer, who was sitting by the roadside, lost in thought. When I told him about the knapsack, he looked contemptuously blank, and I could have sworn at him for not swearing.

We rode on towards Dordon, and before long came to a cottage on the left with a good green paddock beside it. The door was opened by a dark-haired woman wearing a large brooch with an inscription in Welsh. I asked if we could turn the ponies into the field. She replied that her husband was out, and she did not think he would allow it, as they were saving the grass for calves. She suggested another farm on the right, and regretfully we trekked on. There must be a number of colliers from South Wales who have been driven by hard times to seek work in England, and this may account for the Welsh brooch. For Dordon, less than a mile away, is a purely mining village.

We soon reached the turn to the farm indicated. Here we held a council of war. We might push on to Dordon, buy food there, and lunch on the further side. But beyond Dordon, and joined to it, is

Polesworth, and the two straggling villages taken together form a built-up area about two miles in length.
We decided to try the farm. They would surely
have bread and butter, and we could make do with
the tongue. At the end of the lane were two houses,
one quite new, and a block of outbuildings. We saw
an old man pottering in the yard, and made our
usual request. He went off to consult with his son,
and after a while came back and invited us to unsaddle in a large field on the left. Seeing that he was
a friendly old fellow, I told him all about the loss of
the knapsack, and wound up with a tentative request
for bread and butter. This time he went off to consult
his missis, and presently returned with a large plate
piled high with slices of new and thickly buttered
bread. We took this into the field, opened the tin
of tongue with an axe, for the tin-opener was gone
with the knapsack, and fell to, for we were very
hungry.

The field overlooked a shallow valley, with
Watling Street at the bottom. This, unlike the Foss
Way, is now a busy thoroughfare. On the further
side, and at right angles to the main road, the steep
street of Dordon climbed drearily to the sky-line,
bordered by dingy houses and grim industrial places
of worship. The sun had come out, and it was
pleasant to lie on the grass and rest. The prospect
of rousing ourselves to pack and face the transit of
Dordon-cum-Polesworth was far from inviting, but it

was later than usual ; we had lost time over the knapsack, and must push on. The fields of this farm seemed to be all inter-communicating, and when we looked round for the horses, they were nowhere to be seen. While Spencer hunted for them, I went down to the house to pay for the bread and butter. While waiting for change, I noticed in a meadow far below a cob rather like Ladybird. I was just going to comment on the likeness of their pony to ours when another appeared, suspiciously like Excalibur. I rushed off to find Spencer, who was far in the opposite direction. In the end we found all three grazing by a stream. The mystery of the open gates was solved. This was the only water on the farm.

Crossing Watling Street we marched wearily up the hill. Women stood at their doors and watched us pass, but without greeting. Half-way up the street was the post-office, where I sent off a wire and bought some provisions for to-morrow. Coming out, I found Spencer surrounded by the usual crowd of children. There was to be a fair at Polesworth on the following day, and nothing that Spencer could say would persuade them that we were not bound for it. Excalibur's pack must surely contain something saleable or amusing, and it was not until we passed the fair-ground that the children lost their faith and left us. There were various remarks about " Arabs " — the Midland youth is well enough informed to connect pack-animals with nomadism — and a sinister swaying of the load suggested to them, as to us, that something might shortly work loose or fall.

They were not far wrong. We had climbed to the top of Dordon, and were just dropping down the other side into Polesworth, when the load slipped to a dangerous angle, and we had to haul Excalibur to the roadside for readjustment. It was long since we had had any trouble of this kind, and were surprised and duly humiliated. The cause of the trouble was the white kitbag, which contained two rucksacks of different weights, and was in consequence ill-balanced. We always allowed for this in loading ; but the baggage rope, which was nothing better than a Woolworth clothes-line, was getting frayed, and having been shortened to inadequacy, was doubtless to blame for the shift. Our original followers had been youngsters let out early from school, but these were now joined by an ever-increasing throng of older ones, for the schools were now disgorging their huge unoccupied mobs, ready to fall upon the intriguing spectacle of a pack-horse in trouble.

We got the load adjusted, and succeeded in passing the fair-ground, where the rabble, disappointed of their fun, abandoned the chase and went home to tea. But we were hardly clear of the village before the same thing happened again. This time we led Excalibur into a vacant building plot, and repacked from the beginning. At the north end of Polesworth was a bridge over the L.M.S. main line. A very long

goods train was approaching, noisily belching clouds
of smoke, and the horses showed signs of nervousness.
They also disliked the light-coloured paint-work of
the bridge itself. As I watched the line curving away
towards Stafford, I thought that in four or five hours'
time the night express to Scotland would pass this
spot, and any sensible traveller would be sitting at
ease in a comfortable compartment instead of walking
the world with a trio of horses.

As soon as we cleared Polesworth and the railway,
we plunged into the most rural surroundings, which
continued unbroken to the Trent. We could still
hear the distant roar of traffic on the main roads, but
the by-ways were empty, and the only mechanisms
in evidence were numerous and noisy tractors. In
one field, where a lighter type of cultivator was being
towed and the tractor could move pretty fast, a dog
was trotting up and down with the machine. He
had no doubt been accustomed to follow a team of
horses at a walk ; but the mechanisation of farming
had forced him to quicken his pace.

The country was fairly level, with far blue distances. Church spires were stumpier, and large trees
less frequent. The hedges were all of whitethorn,
which makes a less efficient fence than the black
variety, as it has fewer prickles, and a sparser habit
of growth, and is apt to get thin at the bottom. We
noticed the reappearance of harebells by the roadside,
an indication of lighter soil. Towards evening we

had a distant view of the twin spires of Lichfield, veiled in a soft golden mist. We passed through Clifton village, and descended into a shallow valley with a slow-moving river. We had an idea that this stream formed the boundary between Warwickshire and Derbyshire ; and it looked a pleasant place for a camp. Just ahead was a man driving a herd of cows into a field on the right. He had come out of a yard close by, which adjoined an old mill-house. We asked for grazing and got it. He told us that some people had camped in this field last summer, and showed us the remains of their hearth and wood-pile. The field was large and rich, intersected by winding ditches, and sheltered by clumps of willows and high hedges. We turned the horses loose and pitched our tents under the further hedge, on a gently sloping bank well away from the road.

Then came the question of tea. The farmer said we were welcome to have it, but his wife was out, and would not be back till late, and there was no one at home but himself and his young son. He was quite concerned about this, and then I had an inspiration, and asked him if he would object to our making it ourselves, which seemed much better than waiting indefinitely for the mistress of the house. He thought it a good idea, so we all adjourned to the house, where under the direction of a small boy I found tea, milk, sugar, eggs, butter, bread and the rest of it, laid the table, boiled the eggs, and made tea. The

others had already finished their meal, so they sat
and entertained us while we ate. The small boy was
set to chop sticks for the fire, while his father talked
of his experiences in the war. The place had formerly
been a mill as well as a farm, and had remained in
the same family for several generations. The field
where we had pitched our tent was actually in
Derbyshire, so we should fulfil our intention of
sleeping that night in a new county.

Later the farmer's wife came in, and I apologised
for making free with her food and crockery. This
did not seem to worry her at all, and she only hoped
that we had found all we wanted. As we talked, I
noticed for the first time a certain northern inflection
of speech.

We spent some time by the fire, and it was dark
when we left. But the stars were shining brightly,
and by their light we found the field gate, and groped
our way through long grass to our tents. Some care
was needed to avoid the windings of the ditches,
which were narrow and half hidden by bushes and
rank vegetation. We heard the horses munching, and
caught a glimpse of dark shapes among the willows
by the river. This was one of our best camps. The
night was fine, still and mild ; we had a comfortable
pitch, and the agreeable sense of being well up to
time and through the worst of the traffic. To-morrow
morning we should cross the Trent, from which it
was about eleven days' march to the Border.

VIII

Derbyshire

(1) Friday, Sept. 23 — Clifton to Church Broughton

THE day dawned clear and hot, but before long the heat became oppressive, and droves of small curdled clouds appeared from nowhere, promising thunder. We started in good time, and rode through quiet by-ways towards the bridge at Walton, by which we hoped to cross the Trent without passing through Burton. In the distance we saw its chimneys, and those of Ashby-de-la-Zouche, but the country immediately around us was as unspoilt and rural as anything yet encountered. Our baggage rope was daily getting weaker and shorter, and caused a certain amount of slipping of the load. But with only two more pack-horse marches, it seemed hardly worth replacing, even if we had a chance to buy another. We met little traffic but farmers' cars, and these, being driven by men who understand horses, are always easy to pass.

Unfortunately I cannot drive a car myself, so that my experience of motoring problems is one-sided.

Derbyshire

On the road, I am either a driver of shy mountain sheep, or a leader of nervous horses, or a weary pedestrian, smothered with dust or spattered with mud or choked with fumes, and thus may be excused for having a bias. But I must say that nearly all the motorists we met on this long journey showed great consideration, and whatever they did amiss was not through callousness, but from ignorance. There are one or two suggestions I would make. When approaching a restive horse, slow down gradually, and without screaming of brakes. Pass fairly slowly but do not crawl, or the horse will think you are waiting to pounce. Above all, do not accelerate until you are well clear. More horses have been scared by the sudden acceleration of cheap noisy cars than by the smooth passage of a good model at 50 m.p.h. In short, never be sudden in dealing with animals.

We called at Walton post-office for letters, but none were there. A second mail was expected in the afternoon, but having no time to wait for this, we pushed on towards Barton and Tutbury. The road was refreshingly quiet, for the bridge at Walton was not fit for heavy weights, and most of the north-bound traffic crossed the Trent at Burton. The river was broad, turbid, and very swift. On either bank were wide flat water-meadows full of cows, and ditches bordered with willows and poplars. The bridge was guarded by heavy wooden rails, painted white, which continued for some distance along the road. On the north bank and well back from the river was a range of low wooded hills, towards which we slowly made our way, for it was very hot. We had crossed one of the biggest rivers in England, a major milestone, and on the day we intended, and so may be pardoned for being rather pleased.

After a time we came to the large residential village of Barton. The shop at Walton had not looked very promising, and I decided to risk the chance of finding something better further on. At Barton I saw a large co-operative store, where I bought a quantity of good stuff, including some kind of lemon drink in a bottle. The food was packed in a brown-paper parcel and slipped inside one of the kitbags. We were much stared at here — more perhaps than anywhere else, but mercifully the children were in school, and we had no followers.

The road from Barton to Anslow ran at the foot of low hills, shaded by lofty trees, and offering here and there a glimpse of a large farm or country house. On the right-hand side were wide fields which sloped gradually to water-meadows by the Trent. We saw a field of barley still uncut, but several farmers were busy carting dung.

After a forced halt to adjust the pack, we began to look about for a place to rest and eat. The fields were all large and unpromising, but we noticed a lane on the right, about 150 yards long and ending in a gate, to which the horses could be hitched for un-loading. It was not a good pitch, but time was passing, and we must make it do. The lane ran be-tween two hedges, in front of which were ditches with a trickle of muddy water at the bottom. The banks were too deep and the water too shallow to let the horses drink, and we had to water them in an adjoining field. Our corn was finished and there was not much grass, so that the poor creatures, annoyed by the flies that always herald thunder, roamed up and down the lane without stopping for more than a minute in any one place. We took it in turns to herd them, and our lunch, which with the good provisions and lemon drink might have been a festive occasion, was spoilt by perpetual interruption. The sun had gone, but the heat was still oppressive, and now and again, from a veiled and leaden sky, a few large drops would fall. We were in for a storm, I thought, or at least for a drenching downpour.

The water in the ditch was hardly enough to rinse our mug and pannikins. Catching the horses, we began to pack, watched by a large Angus bull, whose placid good-tempered face reminded me of my long-lost and much regretted George of Achnabo.

We marched towards Anslow, seeing nothing of note but another herd of Blue Albions and a park with deer. In the village we ran into more gaping school children, and also met a cart loaded with crockery — no doubt " seconds " from the Potteries.

My Kingdom for a Horse

The march from Anslow to Tutbury was a rather dreary affair. The country was hilly enough to tire the sweating horses, without yielding anything of special interest or beauty, especially when drained of colour by the murky light. There was no freshness in the air, and we felt cross and dejected. Thundery heat is worse for horseback travel than cold or even rain.

Tutbury lies in a valley, and we approached from the south down a long and slippery hill. Just outside the town it began to rain in torrents, forcing the extra burden of a heavy mackintosh. The sheepskin was drenched before I had time to turn it. We found a corn merchant, but only bran was available. While Spencer was seeing it weighed, I put the cover on the pack, watched by the usual crowd of children. I had hardly finished when the rain stopped as suddenly as it began ; but no coolness had come with it, and we plodded on under a lowering sky.

North of Tutbury, but continuous with it, is the long straggling village of Hatton, which like Street, Dordon, and a dozen other places of the same kind, lies drearily strung out along a busy road. I intended, if possible, to sell Jenny and Excalibur at Ashbourne, and wanted a local paper with particulars of sales and auctioneers. But the newsagents were all on the right-hand side of the road, and what with the heat and flow of traffic, I was too lazy to cross and buy one. They will have it at the next farm, I reflected, and passed on. The street of Hatton was alive with lorries and double-decker buses, and at the top of the village we had to cross the Derby-Uttoxeter main road. Then we struck into by-roads and marched a mile or so, looking out for a place to camp.

Before long we came to a large farm-house at a cross-roads. I went into the yard and spoke to a labourer, who introduced me to the farmer's wife, a youngish, energetic woman who was much interested in us and our doings. We followed her across the road to a paddock of an acre or so, with a big cattle-shelter at the top. The shed was empty, and she urged us to pitch our tents inside, as there would certainly be a storm in the night. But our tents were sound, and we preferred to sleep outside on the grass. So we piled the saddlery in the shed, and pitched the tents in the open near the hedge. A couple of labourers came in and examined our ponies with great interest, and later they were joined by the farmer himself, who had just returned from a sale.

We had tea in the big comfortable kitchen, lit by electricity and with a huge north-country range, all shining with polished brass-work. The blinds were carefully drawn down, as our hostess did not care to see lightning. After tea we had a long talk with the farmer, who milked a large herd of dairy Shorthorns. There was no local paper, but we explained that we were parting company at Hartington, and wanted to dispose of two of our horses. We always cherished a sneaking hope that we might hear of some local farmer who wanted a cob ; but no such luck came our way. We got the name and address of the best auctioneer in Ashbourne, and that was all.

It was pitch dark outside. We saw a glimmer of sheet lightning in the direction of Derby, but no storm came, though the air was close and still. In the valley of Tutbury there was a railway as well as a main road, and the shunting of trains was added to the usual traffic noises of the night. It was strange to think that this was our last camp. We had spent eighteen nights under canvas, and there seemed no reason why we should not spend eighteen more, or eighty for that matter. By this time marching and camping had become so much a matter of habit that we could have continued indefinitely. We had of course been lucky with weather and pitches. No gales had blown down the tents, no deluge had soaked them, no straying beasts had wrecked their contents. Had I continued camping to the Border, my experience would have been different.

(2) *Saturday, Sept. 24 — Church Broughton to Hartington*

We woke to the loud patter of raindrops on canvas, and rose hastily, for it was a good ten miles to Ashbourne, and being Saturday, the auctioneer's

office would close at one o'clock. We had breakfast
in the tent, but otherwise were not worried by the
wet, for we could pack in the shed, which was lofty
enough to shelter the horses for saddling and loading.
By the time we were ready to start the rain had
ceased, but the air was close, and a clammy mist
prevented us from seeing very far. The road was
quiet, and rose very gradually all the way to Ashbourne. Had it been clear, we should have had a
view of distant hills, but the mist prevented us from
seeing anything but trees and hedgerows. We noticed
the increase of typically north-country trees, such as
ash and holly, and the elms had a different appearance
from those of the Midlands. Even the oaks were
beginning to change colour, and for the first time, in
spite of the warmth, I felt a touch of autumn in the
air. We marched with an eye on the time, and had
to cut short our rest spells. About two miles out
of Ashbourne I caught a vague glimpse of a range of
abrupt hills with clumps of trees, which greatly delighted me. Soon after this, Spencer discovered
that he had left his whip in the shed at Church
Broughton. It was the first thing he had ever left
behind, and I must confess to some malicious and
unjustified pleasure.

It was after half-past twelve when we first saw
Ashbourne in the valley below. The approach was
by a long steep hill ; the horses slithered and skidded,
and our progress was maddeningly slow. I had tried

to ring up the auctioneer from an intermediate
village ; but when at last we found the post-office,
which was up a lane and out of sight, we were told
that there was no public telephone. So we must
hope to find him delayed by an accumulation of
week-end business. We got directions, and threading
our way through narrow busy streets, arrived on the
doorstep at 12.55 — a praiseworthy achievement.
The clerk took my name, and told me there were
still two people waiting to see Mr. B. So I arranged
with Spencer to take the horses to the stables of the
White Hart, where I could pick him up when the
interview was over.

I joined the other clients on a bench in the hall.
One was a thin middle-aged woman in black, and the
other a stocky farmer, the most typical John Bull that
I have ever seen in these islands. In a minute or two
the thin woman was summoned upstairs, and for some
time John Bull and I sat talking about the prospects
of war. Then he got his call and I was left alone.

It was at least 1.30 before I was ushered into the
presence. I apologised for keeping Mr. B. from his
lunch, and then plunged into my business. He suggested various sales at which the horses could be
offered, and we finally decided on Derby market,
which was to be held in a fortnight's time. I told
him that we intended to spend the week-end at
Hartington, and he said there would be no difficulty
in leaving the horses there till the day of the sale.

This was a relief, as I could not have spared the time to stay with them and see them through myself. I gave particulars of both cobs, and arranged for them to be sold without reserve. In our position there was no other choice. The traveller who sells his horses at the end of a journey, wherever it may be, must risk a loss ; and it rarely pays to keep them on the chance of a better price later on. The expense and uncertainty are too great.

I returned to the stable of the White Hart, and found the horses comfortably unsaddled and munching corn. Spencer appeared, and we adjourned to a café, where we had a substantial *table d'hôte* lunch. Needless to say we greatly enjoyed the luxury of sitting at a table and having no horses to watch. We found it was fourteen miles to Hartington ; and as we should not get clear of Ashbourne till 3.30 at the earliest, it seemed better to book rooms by telephone, so that it would not matter how late we arrived. There was hilly country ahead, and we did not want to press the horses.

The obvious way to Hartington was by the main road to Buxton ; but we had planned a route by side roads through Mappleton and Thorpe Cloud, which would be quieter and more interesting. Being uncertain about the start of this route from Ashbourne, we made more enquiries, and were sent round by the bridge on the Manchester road, which lost us a mile or two and involved us in much traffic.

My Kingdom for a Horse

The river at Ashbourne is most attractive, clear and swift ; and near the bridge it flows over a succession of weirs. We followed the main road for a short distance, and then turning right, rode on through leafy by-ways towards Mappleton-on-Dove. On the left we passed a signpost to Ilam. It would have been pleasant to explore these limestone valleys, with their woods and running streams, for we had seen nothing as charming since we left the Exe at Cove. At the bridge near Mappleton we noticed a smart car drawn up, and two fishermen packing their rods to go home. They were much intrigued by Excalibur, and asked us many questions about our journey.

For some distance our road ran level among trees, and then began the long ascent to Thorpe Cloud. It was close among the woods, and the horses were sweating profusely. The mist lifted a little, revealing those hills and clumps of trees we had seen from the further side of Ashbourne. These heights, steep as they were, carried good grass, and unlike the hills in the gritstone district further north, were enclosed and cultivated to the top. The stone walls were well built and as yet unblackened by the smoke of industry. We met a fair number of tourists, especially on cycles, but it is surprising how little this part of Derbyshire has been spoilt, when you consider its nearness to large centres of population. The higher fields were strangely empty of stock, which puzzled us a good deal, until we heard that large numbers of cattle from Cheshire come there for the summering, and these no doubt had gone, for it was now the last week of September. There must have been some smoke in the air, for the sheep, mostly half-breeds, were rather grimy.

The horses were feeling the long ascent, and Spencer and I dismounted. Excalibur, who could not be relieved, was beginning to lag, and I was sorry there was no means of letting him know that this was his last march. To-morrow there would be no saddling and loading for him, but the start of a fortnight's holiday in a good field. We passed a farm, and beyond it a big quarry, and at last reached the summit. On a clear day we should have had a wonderful view, but we could see nothing but the nearer hills, with here and there a bold limestone crag. The farms were of the smaller hill type, low stone buildings sheltered by clumps of sycamores. The land was pretty good, but it must be bitterly cold and exposed in winter. As we descended towards the valley, we saw a large herd of Frisian cows.

At the bottom we turned left, along the Ashbourne-Buxton main road. This road, which for some distance follows the railway, was not very busy ; it was Saturday evening, and we met nothing but a few touring cars and cyclists. It was now nearly seven o'clock, and heavy clouds were bringing an early dusk. There was so little wind that the smoke from the I.C.I. lime-works spread overhead in a black curtain, smothering the remains of daylight. Further down the line were one or two other mills, but at this point we turned left along a by-road to Hartington.

We had not gone far before it began to rain. We covered the pack and plodded on in our waterproofs. A drove of cyclists passed at full speed, no doubt making for the Youth Hostel at Hartington. Darkness fell, and the rain increased to a steady downpour. But we did not care : our rooms were booked at the inn, and we were sure of supper, beds, and grazing for the horses. We had no idea of the lie of the land, and could only assume that a cluster of lights ahead was Hartington, as indeed it was. This is a big village, and there are several inns beside the Charles Cotton, where we intended to stay. It was not easy to read the signs in the dark, but we found the place in the end. Our last march together, like our first, was ending very late, and we were tired and soaking wet. But we had arrived, and that was the main thing.

We astonished the maids, who were accustomed to the dumb endurance of cars and cycles, by insisting on attending to the horses before we had supper ourselves. There was a good stable, where we un-saddled, and left the trio with a big feed of corn. Later Spencer went back and turned them into a field for the night. We washed and tidied as best we could, and came down to an excellent supper. It was late in the season, and the inn was not very full. We had hot baths, and I confess that I did not read much of *The Worst Journey*. In five minutes I thrust it under my pillow and fell asleep.

(3) *Saturday, Sept. 24, to Monday, Sept. 26*
Hartington Interlude

On Sunday morning we slept very late. When you have come to a new place after dark, there is always a thrill in drawing back your curtains at daybreak, and in seeing if the surroundings are at all as you expected them. But now there was no means of judging, for everything was wrapped in thick mist, and all I could see was the hotel garden, and a corner of the paddock with Ladybird grazing, and the low white buildings of a milk factory. After breakfast I wrote letters, brought my diary up to date, and worked out my route north for several days in advance. I had not got a complete set of maps for Yorkshire and Cumberland, since at the time of ordering, two or three sheets were not available in the new edition. I wrote an urgent letter to Southampton, asking for the missing sheets to be sent, in any style or edition, to the post-office at Meltham, near Huddersfield, which I expected to pass in three days' time.

Just before noon the mist lifted, and we had a good view of the hilly wooded country round Hartington.

My Kingdom for a Horse

The sun came out, and I got leave to hang up our tents on the hotel washing-line in the garden. I also turned out the contents of all the bags and valises and did some washing and mending. These week-end halts, when we had not to think of travelling or getting food, were invaluable not only for rest, but for any kind of business — correspondence, washing, repairs, or repacking — and with our inexperience of horseback travel we could hardly have managed without them.

In the afternoon we tackled the baggage. Spencer was catching a Monday morning train at Buxton, and he agreed to send off the pack-saddle and my own camping equipment to Scotland. My few personal things were packed in a rucksack, and to avoid possible trouble in getting a bed, I kept my blanket, sleeping-bag, and air-mattress, which could easily be carried on the saddle. A few things of little or no value were left behind, including the big blue-enamel teapot in which tea had been made at Newton for over three years.

Later we went to see the horses, and I took photographs of Jenny and Excalibur. I had arranged with the manageress to board them until the day of the sale, when they would be taken to Derby by lorry. Returning to the inn, we found the whole place in a buzz. Cyclists were skimming through the village in flocks, like migrating birds. Never have I seen so many at one time, or in such brilliant array, or moving so quickly. A couple of private buses had just arrived, disgorging forty or fifty sturdy Yorkshire people, who filled the big dining-room with cheerful talk and laughter, and at the end of tea they sang " On Ilkley Moor " by way of national anthem.

I knew that there were letters and a registered envelope shut up in the post-office, and first thing on Monday morning I called to get them. The postmaster was out delivering the mail, but the girl in charge gave me a bundle of letters, and assured me most definitely that no registered envelope had arrived. This was awkward, for the settlement of my hotel bill would leave me without much change. However, I waited for the postmaster to come back, and after some hunting about, he handed me the longed-for sealed envelope. In country post-offices, where they are not accustomed to *poste restante* arrangements, it is as well to insist on a thorough search for any letters that may have been waiting a day or two, thrust aside somehow and forgotten.

I returned to find Spencer's car at the door, and helped him stow away the various packages he was taking to the station. The car whisked round the corner, and I went in to pack for the road, feeling rather sad and lonely. One man and two horses were gone at a blow, and Ladybird and I had still 200 miles ahead. The threat of war grew daily more imminent ; and though I could never persuade myself that any responsible statesmen would be crazy enough to order the death of civilisation, some incalculable wave of popular passion or panic might force them into it, and that would be the end.

(4) *Monday, Sept. 26 — Hartington to Chinley*

I went into the field, looked for the last time at Jenny and Excalibur, and then led Ladybird into the stable. My own saddle and bridle fitted her reasonably well. I strapped the mackintosh and corn-bag to the front dees, and the sleeping-bag and mattress, tightly rolled in the blanket, to the rear ones, and then with the rucksack slung on my own back, was ready for the road. I intended to make for Buxton by way of Hindlow, and then skirting the town, go north towards Chapel-en-le-Frith and Chinley. The air was close in the valley, and as there was a long hill out of Hartington, I led the mare to the summit. Soon the sky cleared and the sun came out ; there was a mountain freshness in the breeze, and the rest of the day was perfect. I mounted Ladybird with alacrity, but forgetting the swing and weight of the rucksack, landed not on the saddle, but on the ground beyond. This did not worry Ladybird, or myself either, for the mare was well-shaped, and there was no trouble with saddle-slipping. Rolling limestone hills, covered with rich green grass and striped with stone walls, lay all around ; there were steep valleys with trees, and in the blue distance a cliff-like escarpment of crags. It was wonderful to be riding with no led horse and so little baggage, free as air, and with no one to consider but our two selves. I even had the energy to dismount and take one or two photographs.[1] There were a few sheep and Shorthorn cattle in the fields, but again the country seemed strangely empty of stock.

We came to the ridge above Hindlow, and the scene changed with a suddenness characteristic of the North, where you pass at one step from moorland solitude to the hum of industry. The abrupt fantastic heights, with their clumps of trees, were replaced by hills that looked higher, bleaker, and more rounded. The landscape was dotted with limeworks, and in the north-west the outskirts of Buxton could be seen. In the wide valley below was a railway and several busy roads, with more mills and houses. There was much noise of blasting, both far and near, and at Hindlow itself we passed a large lime-works, though not at close enough quarters to alarm the mare.

Further on were more works, and a straggling industrial village, with a pub at which I hoped to get tea or cider. But on closer inspection I did not care for it, nor was there any place to leave Ladybird, so I plodded on towards the town. I had a meat pie and chocolate in my pocket, and wanted to find a farm before becoming involved in suburbs. Seeing a lane on the right with a promising farm at the

[1] See frontispiece.

end, I rode up and asked for midday grazing and a drink for the mare. The fields were streamless, and I was shown a trough of water in the yard. To my annoyance and surprise, for it was a hot day, Ladybird sniffed at the water and refused to drink. I turned her loose in a field, and sitting under the lee of a wall, began to eat my lunch. I was still enjoying the peace and freedom of being alone, and the pleasure of riding a good pony. The rucksack was a nuisance, but it was fairly light, and I soon became accustomed to it. I was just thinking of packing up to go, when I saw a woman coming across the field with a tray. She thought I must be thirsty and would like some tea. There was a lace tea-cloth on the tray, a pot of tea, fine china, and a plate of chocolate biscuits ; I was delighted and grateful, but felt deplorably unworthy and shabby. All payment was refused, and I continued my journey in good heart.

My troubles now began. A 1-inch map is difficult to follow in an urban district, because of the network of unnamed roads, and I should have to ask for directions. I wanted to leave the town in a north-westerly direction, without passing through the centre, and then find a bridle-path across the moors to Chapel-en-le-Frith. But each enquiry for the golf-links, a useful landmark, led me further into the town, until I found myself in a long residential road with no one to direct me but a decrepit-looking bath-chairman. He plunged into a long rambling confusion of advice, so helpful in intention, but worse than useless in practice. He even left his bath-chair to accompany me to the turning. But either he misdirected or I misunderstood, for I found no golf-links, but only a dreary collection of boarding-houses. I stopped and made another attempt on the map. From my present position it seemed better to abandon the golf-links and follow the road to Manchester for a mile or two, and then turn right.

The road was uphill all the way, and crowded with traffic, especially with lime-lorries, which Ladybird always disliked. But her shying was less frequent and much less alarming than Jenny's, being caused by rawness rather than by devilment. It was very hot, but I was so glad to get clear of the decayed gentility of Buxton, that I hardly noticed the weariness of the march. Near the top of the hill, the road was under repair, and a gang of men were working with a lorry. I asked for the bridle-path. They were much interested in the mare, and far more helpful than the bath-chairman had been. I took the turning indicated, and found myself in a steep stony lane, which soon emerged upon the open moor. There was a wide view west and south over rolling barren hills, and, far below, the Manchester road descended in zigzags, from which a continuous roar went up. I met nothing on the bridle-path but a few grubby sheep.

For a while we rode on the moor, and then came

to a gate leading into an enclosed lane, which after passing an isolated farm-house, divided in two. The right hand descended very steeply into a wide valley. The hills on this side of the pass were blacker and wilder, and there was little cultivation on higher ground. We slithered down an immensely steep and stony slope, the last place in which one would expect to encounter any kind of motor vehicle. So that I was amazed to hear a chugging noise behind, and turning, saw a lorry overtaking me. The mystery was explained. It was fitted with caterpillar wheels, by means of which it ran gaily over ground that even the riderless Ladybird found difficult to tackle without slipping. Near the bottom was a disused quarry with a fine growth of grass at the entrance. While Ladybird grazed I studied the map. The rest of the route was easy : there was a big reservoir ahead, and then the main road to Chapel-en-le-Frith, and just before reaching the town, a left turn to Chinley. I have a great liking for the reservoirs of Derbyshire and Yorkshire. Not only do they lend charm to a hill country which is curiously lacking in natural lakes, but they make excellent and easily recognisable landmarks.

Leaving the quarry, we passed through a pleasant and fertile valley dotted with residential houses. This part of Derbyshire is easily reached from Manchester and other Lancashire towns, and gives country-loving business people a chance of living away from their work. Every valley has its railway line with frequent trains, as well as good roads. When studying the map, I had noticed that there was a smithy at Chinley ; and as Ladybird's shoes were now much worn, I wanted to get a new set put on before we went any further. Just outside the village I met some roadmen, and made enquiries about the blacksmith. They said he rarely opened his shop before ten in the morning, so I decided to wait till we reached Glossop, where I expected to arrive about dinner-time on Tuesday.

We descended a long hill into the village of Chinley, which lies in a steep valley with a busy railway line at the bottom. On the way down was a trough of cold clear water at which Ladybird condescended to drink. Now that the tent had gone, the problem of the night's lodging was more complicated. Grazing for Ladybird would be more easily found in the open country, and a bed for myself in the village, so that we must make up our minds to be separated. The pony would be best left at a farm on the road we intended to take in the morning ; so I rode right through the village, and enquired at the first place I saw on the road to Hayfield. This proved to be a cottage without land, and I was directed to a farm rather further up on the right. Here they showed me a very small paddock, hardly more than a grass plot, with a not very adequate fence. I wondered if Ladybird would stay there, and was not surprised to hear in the morning that she had broken into the next field. I asked the farmer if he could put me up as well, but he couldn't; and I was recommended to try a little café near the station, where they provided bed and breakfast. There was a fair-sized hotel in Chinley, but I did not fancy their prices, and felt too shabby for hotel company, if it could by any means be avoided.

I found the café, but the beds were all occupied. However, they could give me tea, and afterwards would try to fix me up at another house. The proprietress was out, but the tea was made by her husband and served very competently by two small girls who entertained me with conversation while I ate. They were desperately interested in Ladybird, and longing to cut school in the morning so as to be able to see us off. As soon as I had finished tea, we went out to look for lodgings, and were joined outside by two or three other little girls, so that I had quite an escort. The first two houses were no use, but at last we found a couple living alone with a bedroom to spare. Their children were away, and they were quite glad of company. We sat for a long time chatting by the fire. The man was of the old-fashioned country type, rather quiet and slow ; his wife, who was much quicker and better educated, did most of the talking, and corrected her husband whenever he pronounced a word wrongly or made any kind of mis-statement. He got rather tied up over the word " Czechoslovakia ", and she told him with some asperity that it was time he learned how to pronounce a name so often in the news. Then the wireless was turned on, and later we had some supper. At last I was taken to a very clean and smart bedroom.

Congratulating myself on my luck, I opened the rucksack to look for my diary and *The Worst Journey*. Neither of them was there. I felt rather blank. The Penguin book could easily be replaced, and anyhow I had the second volume to go on with. But the diary was another matter. I have not a good memory, and the details of the earlier part of our ride were growing rather dim. *The Worst Journey* had undoubtedly been left under my pillow at Hartington. But the diary might have been put by mistake into the kit-bag I had sent to Scotland, but more likely had been thrown away by the chambermaid with the superfluities I had left behind. It was written in a shabby, damp-stained Woolworth exercise-book, and no one would suppose it to be of the smallest value.

It was not very late, and I remembered seeing a telephone kiosk in the road quite near the house. I collected a suitable amount of small change, and went out. These kiosks are hateful ; even in the daytime they make you feel like an exhibit in a glass case, and by night it is ten times worse. I stood there in the glare, feeling that all Chinley must be laughing at the idiot who had left a diary behind. But my luck was out. When at last I had put in all the necessary

pennies and sixpences, and pressed Button A and all
the rest of it, I found that I had got the wrong
number. Having no more change for another call,
I fled from the kiosk to drown my sorrows in the
second volume of Cherry-Garrard. But this did not
console me much, for I had been in the middle of
the exciting chapter on the Winter Journey, and
wanted to finish it. I scribbled the day's doings on
an odd sheet of paper and, thoroughly disgusted,
fell asleep.

(5) *Tuesday, Sept. 27 — Chinley to Holmbridge*

I woke to a close and gloomy morning. The hills
were veiled in a mist that threatened to turn to
drizzle, and it looked as if I should see very little
of the beauties of the High Peak. I had a good breakfast, and then strolled up the hill to recover Ladybird.
She was standing alone at the gate, and whinnied with
pleasure when she saw me. She must have been
missing the other horses, and from time to time I
had wondered how she would settle down without
them. But unlike Martha, who always went into
hysterics if left for a moment by herself, Ladybird
had a most philosophic temperament, in which she
resembled my dearly loved and much regretted Joey.
When I led her out of the field at Hartington, where
Jenny and Excalibur were grazing, she never looked
back, nor did she show any surprise or annoyance

at travelling alone on the roads. I gave her a good grooming and feed of oats, and strapped on my roll of bedding, thankful that the packing and loading could now be done in two or three minutes. Neither was I troubled with food to carry, as I intended to have lunch at a café in Glossop while Ladybird was at the smithy. We rode uphill for a mile or so, and then emerged on the main road to Glossop. There was no chance of avoiding a major road, for it was the only possible way North across the High Peak. To find one's way on horseback across these steep and lonely hills, in misty weather without a guide, would have meant endless loss of time ; especially as the land is not unfenced as in most parts of Scotland, but divided into huge enclosures by solid stone walls. But the road was comparatively quiet, and we made good progress. Views there were none. The threatened drizzle had set in, and Kinderscout, which according to the map should be close above us on the right, was hidden in clouds.

Presently we came to Hayfield. This is no rural hamlet, as the name would suggest, but a grim, stone-built industrial village, almost large enough to be called a town, with two or three decayed cotton mills. It had some well-stocked shops, one of which displayed cheap and good bananas, which to me were irresistible. Hitching up Ladybird at the post-office, I made another attempt to get into touch with Hartington. *The Worst Journey* had been found, but no diary : they promised to look for it, and send both books to Haworth post-office. I felt rather dejected, for they must by this time have turned out the bedroom, and if the diary was still missing, there was not much hope for it.

I continued my journey. The drizzle stopped, but it was still thick and misty, and the hills about our road could be inferred rather than seen. An exasperating feature of travel in Britain is the way in which good weather haunts the dullest districts, while as soon as you come to anything worth seeing, down comes the mist or a squall of rain, and all is lost. Not quite all, for there are often gleams of light, and things half seen among clouds ; but that morning there was nothing. Presently we came to Charlestown, a suburb of Glossop, with mills and rows of stone cottages. There was nothing new here. Both mills and houses looked as if they dated from the earliest days of the industrial revolution, and in their solid plainness, so much in keeping with the wild surroundings, had, like the Cornish mines, a kind of historic dignity. But there is more than a chance that these mills, again like the Cornish mines, have seen their day. The Glossop district is now a distressed area, and no one I spoke to had much hope of a revival of the cotton trade, especially in smaller and less central places.

Half-way through Charlestown street was a mill from which a jet of steam puffed horizontally across the road. Ladybird took one look at it, and then stopped dead. No coaxing, exhortations, or blows would induce her to advance a step. A cart overtook us, drawn by a horse to whom jets of steam were nothing. I dismounted, and tried to lead her on beside the other horse. But it was useless. At last I backed her past the nuisance. It took some time, but was quite effective. I then enquired for a blacksmith.

The smithy was large, and stood well back from the road. There was another horse before us, so I left Ladybird while I went to get some lunch. The place seemed unnaturally quiet, and to my great surprise I found that it was early closing day. Tuesday is an unusual and unsatisfactory day to choose, being so near to Sunday, but as the waitress remarked, " We're used to it, and don't notice it." The grim little town had many unemployed, and the inhabitants went about with rather a careworn look, but they were full of friendliness and of that stoical good-humour with which North Country people so often meet and lighten trouble.

After lunch I returned to the smithy, an up-to-date workshop with an electric bellows. The blacksmith said that this bellows was useful, and good enough for ordinary jobs like shoeing horses, but he had much to do with the repairing of machine parts, and when he wanted really fierce heat, the big hand-worked bellows were the best. He had already put two shoes on Ladybird, who stood very quietly. She was afraid of the smoke and sizzling when the red-hot iron was fitted, but the smith hung his cap on her ear, which prevented her from seeing too much, and all was well. The job was very well done, but it cost nearly twice as much as I should have paid in the South.

We climbed out of Glossop on the way to the Woodhead reservoirs. The sun had begun to struggle through the clouds, which as they rolled away from the hills, revealed a scene reminiscent of the central Highlands. On the western side of the road I noticed a few scattered houses and mill chimneys ; but north and east were high empty hills, seamed with infrequent stone walls. After a quiet ride of three or four miles we came in sight of the long chain of reservoirs which supply water to Manchester. The whole system is about seven miles in length, and occupies the bottom of a deep and lonely valley. The charm of this place, which has all the wild beauty of a Highland lochside, is spoilt by a railway line, where labouring strings of trucks pass every few minutes, and by the ceaseless stream of traffic on the Manchester-Sheffield main road, which runs on the north side of the water. Every stream that flowed down from the hills was guarded by Corporation notices forbidding you to meddle with it. The trains kept darting in and out of short tunnels with a screech of whistles, and at one point was a level

crossing where we had to wait for a time till the
gates were opened. The different sections of the
reservoir were connected by channels regulated by
sluices. Near the eastern end our road crossed to the
north side and joined the main road. There was a
bad half mile along the crowded and noisy thoroughfare, until we reached the Woodhead Inn and turned
left towards the pass that leads into Yorkshire. This
road was deserted, and we had a good rest before
tackling the ascent, which is nearly two miles long
and at the summit reaches a height of about 1700
feet.

We crossed a narrow bridge with a hairpin bend
above it, and followed the road, which wound in
ever-ascending spirals into the heart of the hills.
Turning a bend, we lost sight of the main road, and
the diminishing roar of traffic was drowned in the
brawling of a stream a hundred feet below. Somewhere on this climb we walked into Cheshire and
out again, but I am not sure where, and it does not
matter very much. The scene might have been
almost anywhere in the mountainous parts of Britain
— rock and coarse grass, heather and bracken and
running water. The sights and sounds of the hill,
and the clean pure air with its moorland scent re-
vived me, and I plodded on, leading my willing and
companionable mare. The summit was not a ridge,
but a wide tussocky plateau of moss, which must
have been rich in peat. But the inhabitants have too

much coal at hand to bother with turf-cutting, especially at such an altitude.

We began to descend. On a clear day there would have been a fine view to the north and east ; but the distances were still veiled in mist, and I could not see much beyond the nearer valleys, which were cultivated and dotted with houses. In a steep hollow on the right the spreading smoke-haze and slender chimneys of Holmfirth were just visible. My plan was to give this town a miss, and continue by Holmbridge to Meltham and Marsden, and thence, avoiding Slaithwaite, to Mytholmroyd.

The descent was long and tiring, and left me shaky in the knees. I intended to sleep at Holmbridge, which was not much further on ; and as I passed through the village at the bottom of the pass, I asked a man if he knew of anyone in that direction who would put up my pony. He indicated a house on a hillside about two miles further on. It was getting late, and I was annoyed to find that we were separated from the farm by one of those steep narrow valleys so characteristic of this part of Yorkshire, which, running east and west across the track, make every northward leading road seem twice as long as it is. We stumbled down a stony cart-track and found at the bottom a half-demolished mill. The valley had been bought by some neighbouring town council for a new reservoir ; and I heard complaints about this, for the mill was still in action, and gave local employment.

Derbyshire

We toiled up the other side, and found ourselves on a steep slope, dotted with small farms. The houses were built on a uniform pattern which prevails through a large district of the West Riding. Many of them were inscribed with initials and dates, which showed that they belonged to the last quarter of the eighteenth century. The roof was made of oblong stone slabs, and the walls of four-square masonry, the whole house being of such fortress-like solidity that if the main timbers were renewed, it would have every chance of outlasting the beehive huts of pre-historic man. There was a central deep-set door, flanked by two heavily mullioned windows with three or four lights in each, and on the upper floor, three more windows also mullioned. Under the same roof, and often rather larger than the house, was a barn, with an enormous arched doorway through which you could drive a loaded waggon of hay or corn. In the fields were a few cattle, and a very large number of fowls, some housed in home-made shacks, others in arks and modern free-range houses. The growth of industry has turned rural Lancashire and West Yorkshire into one vast chicken-run, and poultry farming with a little dairying is the chief occupation of all these small-holders. There is always a temporary ramshackle look about poultry appliances, however well made, and they were in startling contrast with the grim rock-like solidity of the dwelling-houses, each a potential Wuthering Heights.

My Kingdom for a Horse

I reached the farm indicated and found the farmer, a pleasant-faced young fellow who took in Ladybird without a moment's hesitation. There was no bed for me, and he directed me to a pub about half a mile away. It looked a pleasant enough place, and had " ACCOMMODATION " painted in large letters on the wall. But when I asked for a bed and breakfast, they assured me that they had no bedroom, and could not even give me tea. There was, they said, a Youth Hostel another half mile further on, where I should no doubt get a bed. Weary and cross, I plodded down the road, knowing that every step I advanced was taking me further from Ladybird, and would have to be retraced in the morning. I began to long for the independence of the tent, though I dread to think what would have become of the pack-horse on these switchback hills. Nor was the prospect of a Youth Hostel very cheering. Being thoroughly undemocratic, I hate sharing a room, and had visions of a dormitory full of ebullient young women. But my fears were groundless. The holiday season was practically over, and no one went to this hostel except at the week-end. It was a fair-sized converted country villa, and I was offered a large bedroom, with the choice of five beds. I had a magnificent hot bath, and tea and talk with the wardens.

After tea I made a long study of maps. The next sheet was a dreary affair — nothing but sprawling towns, with a semi-rural corridor between Huddersfield and Rochdale, which I must negotiate on the next day. After that I should be clear. There was, however, a bewildering network of roads, and if I were not very careful, I should take a wrong turn and get involved in railways or tram-lines. The hostel stood on high ground, and a little further on the western skyline was the Isle of Skye Inn, which claims locally to be the highest inn in England. Actually it is only the third highest, being surpassed by Tan Hill near Brough, and the Cat and Fiddle in Derbyshire.

IX

Yorkshire

(1) *Wednesday, Sept. 28 — Holmbridge to Cragg Vale*

THIS was the worst day I spent on the road. We were on the brink of war ; and in a few hours might be committed beyond hope. The gloom and uncertainty of human minds appeared symbolised by a thick dirty fog, which later turned to rain. I had an early breakfast, and trudged back to the farm for Ladybird. I found her already caught and groomed and saddled, and my host would not take a penny for these services. I left the place at 8.30 — my earliest start — and the church clock was striking nine as I rode into Meltham, a large semi-urban village about five miles from Huddersfield. I went at once to the post-office, where I expected to find the map I had ordered from Southampton. Nothing was there. My last sheet ended three miles north of Haworth, which I expected to reach by noon on Thursday. After that was a blank, until I should reach the district covered by the sheet which contains Kirkby Lonsdale and Hawes. There was no public telephone at the post-office, and so I retired to a nasty little kiosk in the main street, rang up a well-known bookseller at Huddersfield, and persuaded him to forward the map to Haworth post-office without waiting for a remittance. He was naturally loth to send anything without payment to a complete stranger at a *poste restante* ; but by harping on my sad and mapless plight, I made him relent, and when I reached Haworth the right sheet was waiting with the rest of my mail.

Leaving Meltham, whose dreary outskirts sprawled in all directions, I climbed a long hill towards Marsden. The fog was thicker than ever, and I could see nothing but a section of road in front of me. Below on the right appeared to be a valley, containing like most valleys in the West Riding, a river, a railway, a main road, houses, and mills. Somewhere in this valley was Slaithwaite, which I wished to avoid, but whether it was now ahead, abreast or behind I had no idea. Noises, muted by fog, came up from below — noises of trains, of road traffic, of sirens, but too vague and confused to give much help. I wanted to cross this valley somewhere west of Slaithwaite, and then ride by Bradshaw and Pole Chapel to Scammonden. This involved turning right before reaching Marsden ; but there were several right turns, and being by this time thoroughly bewildered, I sought guidance from a group of roadmen. They were most sympathetic, but not as helpful as they might have been, for they all started arguing among themselves, and I had difficulty in persuading them that on no account did I wish to go to Slaithwaite. It was out of my way, and to judge from the noises coming from that quarter, not the kind of place to appeal to Ladybird. Having at last made this clear to them, they indicated a turning a few yards further on, which I followed in hope.

The lane descended in sharp bends, and from the increasing uproar ahead I gathered that it would soon debouch upon the main road. In another five minutes I found myself on the edge of a thoroughfare resembling the Coventry-Birmingham road at Meriden, only with the addition of trams. According to the map, the by-road I was to follow should have been just opposite, involving a mere crossing of the traffic stream. But there was no sign of such a by-road ; and on making enquiries from a friendly greengrocer, I was told that it was a good half-mile further on. But if I wanted to avoid the trams, I could go back by the way I had come, and take a bridle-path on the right that would bring me out quite close to it. So we turned round and plodded up the hill again. The bridle-path started near a large school, and for some distance ran parallel to the tram-lines in a westerly direction ; then it turned abruptly downhill, and narrowing into a kind of stony gorge between high walls, emerged on the main road at a point where it was under repair, with all the traffic crowded

on to one side. Further enquires from workmen
showed that the by-road I wanted was still 300 yards
ahead.

Waiting an opportunity, I crossed the road ; the
pony was getting restive, and in an urban district I
did not care to lead her on the footpath. Then I had
an inspiration. Beside me was a gate leading into the
fields of a poultry farm. The fog was now a little
thinner, and I could see that by cutting across these
fields I should reach the by-road in peace. I opened
the gate boldly and went in. For a time I waited, to
give Ladybird a rest and a feed on the good grass,
and then found my way through three or four enclosures to another gate which led directly to the
by-road. This cross-country journey caused some
delay, for I had to take down and re-erect a couple
of complicated barriers made of wooden bars and
old bed-heads and thorns and wire. But I had gained
my object, and here we were, safely across Jordan.

The hills on the north side of the Slaithwaite
valley are covered with small-holdings, connected by
the usual network of lanes ; and as we crossed the
bridge I was foolish enough to ask the way to Bradshaw, which is not a village, but one of these innumerable upland farms. My informant, a woman,
plunged into the most complicated directions, and
then called in an old man who happened to be passing.
They fell into a heated topographical argument, which
lasted for a long time, until I felt utterly bewildered,

and wished I had had the sense to stick to my map and hold my tongue. Free at last, I climbed another incredibly steep hill. At the top the fog was denser, and after a time it turned to a fine wetting rain. I rode through narrow winding lanes, with farmsteads everywhere, all small and all, as it seemed, exactly alike. Except for industrial noises that floated up from hidden valleys, one might have been in any remote moorland country, and, bar the poultry, at any epoch in the last two hundred years. Flocks of white Leghorns were thick as hailstones in the little fields, and I was told that on most of these upland farms eggs are the chief source of income, and life would be impossible without them.

In the end I found Bradshaw, which was distinguished by a clump of trees, and then at another farm enquired for Pole Chapel. Everyone was very friendly, which in my draggled and forlorn condition cheered me greatly. The Chapel lay on another main road, which I must cross to reach Scammonden and Rishworth. Near the corner was a big co-operative stores, where I bought some bananas and asked if there was any place where I could get lunch. There was a tea-room further on, and close to the stores, I noticed a cottage, with a promising paddock for Ladybird. I went in and asked if I could leave her there for an hour ; and it was not till she was well inside the gate that I discovered that there was no approach to the grass except by a narrow flight of four steps.

The foundations of the house and the flagged path from the gate had been excavated from a sloping field, and the edges banked with stone. No stock was kept, so the problem of access to grazing did not arise. The sunk path was too narrow for turning, and I was about to back the mare out, when she took a step forward, and spying the grass, ran up the steps like a goat and began to graze. So far so good : but how was I going to get her down ? But that could wait. I would have my own lunch before tackling this problem.

The tea-shop proved to be a corrugated-iron annexe to a farm-house, rather like the shack at Maxstoke, but smarter and much larger. There were no other diners, and I prepared to enjoy a quiet meal of ham and eggs, bread and butter, and tea. There was a notice requesting clients to pay on receiving their order, for the annexe was a little distance from the house, and it would be easy enough to abscond without being noticed. But when I produced my ninepence in advance it was waved aside, and I paid after eating as if I had been in an ordinary restaurant. No one need go hungry in this part of Yorkshire ; there are any number of tea-shops of a cheap and democratic variety, even in the most un-likely places.

I did not linger long. It was still very foggy, and I was anxious to get back to Ladybird, for it might take some time to coax her out of the paddock. I caught and led her to the steps, but as I feared, without result. In such a place, uphill is easier than downhill, and there was nothing to tempt her into that narrow flagged path. Corn, sugar, apples were all tried, but in vain. With the assistance of my hostess, I tried to drive her down, but she merely turned skittish and galloped round in circles. What was to be done now ? I had visions of staying there until Ladybird, driven by thirst, came out of herself, or of collecting a gang of men with tackle to haul her out by force. Then I noticed that part of the wall between the paddock and the road was built without mortar, and I asked the owner if I might make a gap, lead the mare through, and build it up again. Permission was given, and I started heaving down the stones, until I had made a breach wide enough to admit a pony. I led her up very carefully ; the place was new, and she was suspicious. But she went, and hitching her to the gate outside, I proceeded to build up the gap. In the west of Ireland this is a common way of moving stock from field to field ; but in Yorkshire it hardly seemed the thing, and I am sure the wall was not improved by such tinkering. But no one objected, and we went on our way without further difficulty.

I have no idea when we entered or left Scammonden : houses were everywhere but without definite grouping or centre. Soon we plunged into another narrow valley, following a roughly cobbled track which was said to be one of the old pack-horse roads. But its steep and slippery surface made me thankful that poor old Excalibur was safe at Harting-ton. This wooded glen, with a brawling stream at the bottom, was empty of mills and houses, and gave me a notion of what the West Riding was like before the industrial revolution. The mist had cleared a little, but it was still raining steadily. We climbed out of the valley and emerged on a stretch of open moor, intersected by artificial water-channels for the supply of some reservoir. Here I met a couple of farmers who, tickled by the appearance of the saddle and rolled blanket, asked me if I were going to the war. I pointed out that I was riding in the wrong direction, and perhaps was running away.

Before long we reached the lip of another valley, on the further side of which were the houses and mills of Rishworth. We crossed the river by a narrow bridge near the old ford, which must once have been used by pack-horse trains. Outside Rish-worth we cut across a main road and followed a minor one to Pike End. Owing to the frequent breakneck hills, much of this day's march had been on foot ; but now we had come to a stretch of easier gradients, and I was once more in the saddle. Some children returning from school walked with me for a while, busily talking. At Pike End we crossed one of the busy thoroughfares that connect Yorkshire and Lancashire, and turned into a road which led across the moors to Mytholmroyd, where I intended to spend the night. Enquiring the distance at a farm by the wayside, I learned that it was not more than six miles.

But my luck was out. The wind fell, and the fog once more dropped low on the hills. Drifting smoke mixed with the heavy clouds to bring a premature darkness. Somewhere near the top of the moor the road forked. I halted irresolutely. My map was of paper — a senseless economy — and with much handling in the rain, was reduced to pulp and tatters. There was no one in sight, and if there were any houses near, they were lost in mist and as good as non-existent. It was getting dark, if not late, and I must do something. I turned left. The road was curving away too far, but it could not be helped. I met a man, who told me to keep straight on for Mytholmroyd, and lower down, a woman at a farm-house told me the same thing. I was still more puzzled when, after a good six-mile ride from Pike End, I came out on a major road at a milestone which read " Mytholmroyd $3\frac{1}{2}$ miles ". I then discovered that instead of approaching the place directly, I had dropped into a lateral valley which must be followed down to its junction with the main valley at Mytholmroyd.

Night was falling and I must find quarters as soon as possible. I rode on, keeping a sharp look-out for farms, but in the steep-sided valleys the cultivated land is on top, and the farm-houses were mostly perched aloft, and approached by lanes on a higher level. My road dropped deeper into a wooded crack in the hills, and the chances of passing a farm seemed very remote. Presently we reached a group of houses, and I asked an old man if he knew of anyone who would put up my pony. He said there was a good inn a little way further down, where I could stay myself, and near it a small-holder who had a field for his poultry, and might consider taking Ladybird.

The tall stone-built inn had a forbidding look. There was no one about, but after a time a man answered my ring. He looked me up and down, and then said that his wife was away, and he could not take me in. He suggested another inn on the further side of the valley. So we turned off the main road, crossed a bridge and found ourselves outside a pleasant-looking country pub. I rang the bell hopefully, and was met by a plump kindly woman who received me at once, and sent her husband to arrange with a neighbouring farmer for Ladybird's grazing. While waiting for his return I gave the mare a good feed, and later, when I had seen her led away to the field she was to share with two heifers, I sat down to a well-earned tea. With various delays I had been marching for twelve hours, and yet without covering the whole distance planned.

My Kingdom for a Horse

(2) *Thursday, Sept. 29 — Cragg Vale to Cowling*

In the weariness of the previous night I had forgotten to name a time for breakfast, and when I rose
at 7.30 the whole place was wrapped in silence. The
kitchen premises were approached by a separate
entrance ; I unlocked the back door and glowered
into the kitchen window from outside, but could see
no one. In the upstairs dining-room was a service
lift. Opening the slide, I called down it. No reply.
Then with the hatch still open I listened, and heard
vague noises, like the grunting and stretching of someone just waking from sleep. I gave another call. It
was answered by my hostess, who appeared very
promptly with many apologies. While she cooked
my breakfast, I went up to the field, caught and
saddled Ladybird, and hitched her to the pillar of the
porch. My bedding had been no use to me, and I
decided to scrap the mattress and sleeping-bag, re-
taining only the blanket in case Ladybird should get
a sore back. I made up a parcel and posted it home
from Cragg Vale. We were now travelling as light
as possible. Leaving the post-office, I rode down
towards Mytholmroyd. I was stopped by a young
woman in a car, who was an enthusiastic horse-lover,
and wanted to know all about the trek. She offered
hospitality, which would have been more than wel-

come the night before. She also gave me directions for finding the old moor road from Pecket Well to Haworth, for which I was very grateful.

I was wearing breeches made in Mytholmroyd, and had often wondered what this oddly named little place was like. Our road merely skirted the town and climbed a steep hill to Midgley. At the top we turned sharp left, and rode high up along the north side of the valley in which lay Mytholmroyd and Hebden Bridge. The mist was gone, and the clearing sky allowed me to see for the first time the country through which I had been travelling. The pattern was everywhere the same : rolling moorland broken by steep wooded valleys, in which, packed close, were mills, railways, and houses. Higher up came the farms, and above these, the open moor. The road was level, and as I was now comparatively free of baggage, we could both enjoy a trot. After a couple of miles we left this road, which descended sharply to Hebden Bridge, and turned right towards Pecket Well. On the way we passed an immense derelict mill, built like a fortress to last all time. It was erected in 1859, and closed down in the slump of 1931. Unless there is some great economic change, it will not be reopened, and in another fifty years will be a picturesque ruin. For there is nothing shoddy about the mid-Victorian mills ; they were built by men who used good material in an honest workmanlike fashion, and in decay need fear no comparison with Roman villas or Norman castles.

A little further on I had a talk with a youngish woman, who with her husband had formerly worked in the mill. Now they were making a living out of poultry, as many other mill hands had been forced to do. I wondered if this were the beginning of a counter-revolution. But if industry goes, there will be no one left to buy eggs. She asked me where I was going, and said that when I first hove in sight, she thought it was the Yeomanry. So much for a military saddle ! I bought a few bananas at a co-operative store, and not long after left the road, which led on to Keighley, and turned into the moor-way to Haworth.

The first part of this road was enclosed, and I passed a number of small hill farms. Goats were plentiful, and I saw two half-grown kids playing on the stone-flagged roof of a dwelling-house. Not far off a heifer was having a friendly scrap with a ram. These farms had comparatively few sheep, because they are difficult to control and invariably cause bad feeling between neighbours. To keep sheep in comfort, you need to be a good mile from the nearest neighbour, or to be ringed with a deer fence six feet high.

Presently we reached the moor. There were fine views in all directions, especially towards Lancashire, for the eastern slopes are broken by the sprawling growth of Keighley and its satellite villages. In the distance the smoke-stacks of Keighley could be seen, and nearer, Oxenhope village and church, and the back of the ridge from which Haworth village straggles down to the valley. Near the reservoir I met a farmer who was out to gather his flock, and we had a talk about sheep, and then about the Brontës, in whom he took much local pride. Their mixed Irish and Cornish descent appears no bar to the patriotic veneration of Yorkshiremen.

I approached Haworth from the west, following a road which ran just above the church and parsonage. The moors immediately behind the village are now spoilt by extensive quarries, and it is not until you are near the Lancashire border that there seems (at any rate in these days) to be anything fit for Emily to walk on. I left Ladybird at a farm on the Colne road, and walked into the village to get my letters. The farmer had described Haworth as a country place, but to one accustomed to emptier lands, it seemed more like a town. I passed through a modern suburb, embellished with a brand-new public convenience, which stood in a trim compound, as if it were the temple of some cult of Health and Hygiene. Near it was a notice advertising the luxury coaches of the Brontë Omnibus Company.

Another five minutes brought me to the top of the old village, with its grim little houses, which must be just as they were in 1840, only the Black Bull has been smartened to receive tourists, and I imagine Branwell would no longer feel at home there. Most of the shops have Brontë souvenirs, and there is a Brontë Café, where I had a good light lunch. Then I climbed a flight of steps and entered the churchyard, which surely has more gravestones to the acre than any burial-ground in England. It was thought crowded a hundred years ago, but on a rough estimate, more than half the stones I saw were erected after the middle of last century. It was a bright day, and the renovated front of the parsonage had mitigated its severity, but the air was dank with yesterday's rain, and the graves drifted over with leaves of sycamore — that gloomy tree whose buds are slow to open, and leaves turn sere before the corn is ripe. In winter time, when sleety winds howl down from the moors and set the branches groaning, it must be grim to walk among so many bones.

I called for my letters. The map had come, and I spread it out on a table in the Brontë Café. My next important stage was Hawes in the extreme north-west of the county, which might be reached by an easterly route through Skipton or a westerly route through Settle. One-inch maps invariably have joins in the most awkward places, and the sheet for Huddersfield just failed to include Skipton. So perforce I decided on Settle, and planned to push on to Cowling, where I would spend the night. There was also a small parcel at the post-office, containing my diary and the missing volume of *The Worst Journey*.

I returned to the farm, where Ladybird was happily grazing with a herd of Shorthorn cows. The field was very muddy, and I had some difficulty in finding a clean place to saddle up. But at last we were out on the Colne road, trotting gaily towards Stanbury, a village about two miles out of Haworth. Here I noticed a large barn standing open to the street, where a couple of labourers were working among bins and sacks of feeding-stuffs. A very old man was sitting before it in the sun, and I asked if they could sell me some oats for the pony. He told me to go in and make what mixture I liked. I took about 25 lb. of oats mixed with flaked maize, for which no payment was accepted. When the old fellow heard I had come from Cornwall and was making for Scotland, he could hardly believe his ears. It appeared that I must follow the Colne road for another six miles before turning north to Cowling. Actually there was a short cut across the moor, but no one recommended it, and after my experience of the previous night, I thought it might be better to stick to the road.

After leaving Stanbury, we began to climb into the wild and desolate country where the West Riding marches with Lancashire. Here were the moors which, without seeing Haworth, one would associate with the Brontës ; but they were a good five miles' walk from the parsonage.

On the western side of the pass the hills dropped

abruptly to the wide, well-populated Colne valley, with a haze of mill-smoke in the distance, and beyond, a long line of empty fells. At the highest point of the road was a small farm and an inn. These hill-top inns are cunningly placed to catch custom, for the traveller, from whichever side he comes, is sure to have developed a thirst. Here I was told that it was two miles or so to Laneshaw Bridge, where I must turn right, and then three and a half miles to Cowling along the Colne-Keighley main road. I heard more of the elusive short cut, but my informant said it was rough and boggy, and I should be sure to lose my way. This was annoying, for the march promised to be a long one, with the last hour spent in leading Ladybird in a roar of traffic. I should be late at Cowling, and it might take some time to find accommodation. To-morrow I should reach a district where tourists are more plentiful, and inns prepared to welcome visitors. But Cowling is not a tourist resort, and my recent experiences had not been very encouraging.

At the bottom of the hill I saw in the distance the Keighley road with cars and lorries speeding along it. There appeared to be a short cut through a farm, by which a mile or so might be saved. But it proved to be a footpath with stiles, and I had to go round by Laneshaw after all.

The march to Cowling was rather like that to Glastonbury, only mercifully I was fresher and had only one horse. There were, however, double-decker buses, and to the end Ladybird detested them. The hills from which I had descended stretched north in long cliff-like escarpments, with a pillar at the highest point. Between them and the road were scattered moorland farms, built in the primitive style, and not quite in keeping with the ultra-modern high-road. Those miles seemed very long ; but at last we reached Cowling, a good-sized village with a derelict mill and a number of prosperous-looking dairy farms. At the entrance to the village was a large gloomy-looking inn called the Black Bull. I looked at it doubtfully. On the door was a notice, " Transport men catered for ". That, I thought, means that people will be coming in and out all night, and lorries will be halted and started up with barbarous noises. I would try somewhere else first. In any case they probably would not fancy an odd-looking female with a horse. So I started to look for a farm. Near the church was a promising place, and it was not too far from the Black Bull if I were unlucky enough to have to go back there.

I rode into the yard. Hearing the clatter of hoofs, the farmer came out from the cow-shed, and we fell into conversation. At the mention of Cornwall he pricked up his ears. It appeared that he had bought two Guernsey heifers from a Cornish dealer who advertised far and wide, and owing to the distance had not been able to inspect them before purchase. I was surprised : he could have obtained Guernseys much nearer home, from local breeders or even at

Crewe market : but such is the power of the printed word ! He offered grazing for Ladybird, and then I tackled the question of a lodging for myself. He suggested the Black Bull, and when I demurred, went in to consult his missis. Among farmers, an aversion from licensed houses is thought a virtue in a woman, and I used this engine for all it was worth. The interview ended as I had hoped, and I was offered a bed in the house. Then we unsaddled and fed Ladybird in the stable, where she was left for an hour or two to cool off.

I heard the too-familiar strains of radio, and to my astonishment found that it came from the cow-shed, where milking was in progress. When I asked if it stimulated the cows to let down their milk, the farmer replied that he had a portable set, and during the crisis they had carried it with them to the cow-shed, so as not to miss any news.

I inspected the herd with the two Cornish heifers, and then went into the house. The plump, good-natured farmer's wife was in the middle of such a baking as only Yorkshire can produce. Bread, buns, cakes, pies were either already made or still in the oven, and every few minutes she would open the door and take out some fresh and fragrant delicacy. I was ravenously hungry, and wondered how long it would be before the others came in, and we could begin to eat a few of these appetising things. " We study our toomies here," the housewife said, and with justice. For another half-hour I lived on hope and aromas, until the family assembled and we fell to.

After tea one or two neighbours came in for milk, including a woman who had read and liked my articles in the *Farmer's Weekly*, and from that I enjoyed a quite unjustified celebrity. Later we were joined by a young man on A.R.P. duty ; and there was much merriment about gas-masks and air-raid precautions in general. The slow-moving countryman is not easily scared, and the idea of hostile aircraft over Cowling was treated with a levity which would have shocked the authorities.

The family had been only for three years in their present quarters, having moved from a bungalow barely three miles away. My hostess complained that the old farm-house was terribly inconvenient, and for a long time the Cowling people treated them as strangers, and stared at them as they went about their work. In spite of modern transport the old clannishness survives. On several occasions I had been surprised to find that people had never heard of a town not ten miles away. And incidentally this was the only district in which I had any difficulty in understanding the local speech.

(3) *Friday, Sept. 30 — Cowling to Kettlewell*

In the morning we heard of the Munich agreement, and I suppose that the gas-masks of Cowling were cast with other farmer's junk into some dusty loft or mildewed barn. Once more I found Ladybird caught and saddled, and again payment was refused ; but in the end I induced them to take something for my board and lodging. I also received much advice about the next stage of my journey, which proved more confusing than helpful. I should have liked to sleep at Kettlewell, where I knew of a good inn, but the village and its approaches were off my Ordnance sheet, and to judge from the small-scale general map, the distance was rather beyond a single day's march. So I decided to go to Settle by Elslack and Gargrave.

On leaving the village, I should have gone by Cowling Hill Lane to the Skipton road. But west of Cowling was the usual network of farm lanes, and, confused by too many verbal directions, I took a wrong turn somewhere, and found myself at a dead end in the middle of a field. Not far off was a house from the door of which an old man was watching me with interest. I trotted up and asked for Cowling Hill Lane. His explanations were in broad dialect, but as he came with me to unfasten the gate, and illustrated his meaning with gestures, I gathered that I must cross a field and ride through a wood, and over two more fields, and then I should be in Cowling Hill Lane. In the first field were two young horses who made circles round Ladybird, and did their best to follow her out of the gate. We soon found the Lane, and turned left to join the Skipton road. Here for some time we played hide-and-seek with a milk lorry, which kept passing and dodging into farm gates, and then would overtake and pass again. It was a nuisance but good practice for Ladybird. The farms here were smaller than those immediately round Cowling, and more of the hill type, but they were mostly devoted to dairying. I saw a few sheep, but not many ; for the mountain and grassland flocks of Yorkshire are mainly in the Dales.

We climbed a hill, at the summit of which was a stretch of heath with woods beyond. The day was fine, and as the air was very clear, I could see the wild moors and fells towards Skipton, and westward, the rolling farmlands through which our own road lay.

Turning left, we made a long descent to Elslack, the first definitely rural village I had passed since leaving Sterndale, between Hartington and Buxton, six days before. And apart from a lime-works near Hetton, and one or two small collieries in the Naworth district of Cumberland, I was to see no more industry. Between Elslack and Gargrave the country was charming — woods and pasture-land with running streams, and purple fells in the distance. In the North the state of the crops is very noticeably a matter of altitude : grain ripens later anyhow, and hills attract the rain that hinders work. In South Derbyshire, a lowland district which had shared in the southern drought, I had found both hay and corn secured. North of the Peak the weather had broken in July, and although on lower ground the hay was saved, everyone was late with the corn. Hill farmers were the least fortunate ; many of them had hay still out in cocks, or even uncut.

On the way to Gargrave I passed a fold where they were dipping a flock of Swaledales, belonging to the owner of a mansion near by. With the disappearance of mills, country-houses were becoming more frequent, and nowhere could they have a more attractive setting. We passed the old church at Broughton, which lay away from the village in a grove of trees. Opposite was a stable erected in the seventeenth century. The fashion of signed and dated buildings still prevails : not far from here I saw a stone barn with the date 1926, and the builder's initials. We crossed a main road, and followed an undulating by-road to Gargrave, a good-sized village with a railway station.

I found a farm for Ladybird on the northern outskirts, and then went back to get some lunch. We were coming into tourist country, and there was no lack of inns and tea-rooms. I selected a quiet café where I had a good and inexpensive meal. The village was full of sheep and shepherds, for it was the season of the sales, and a large consignment had just come in by train. They were Swaledales, with a sprinkling of heavy Wensleydale rams. Most of these were very lame, for the wet weather had favoured foot-rot.

Yorkshire

I called for Ladybird, who was much petted by
the young women of the house. We left Gargrave
by a minor road which skirts the demesne of a large
country-house. There were plenty of trees about
and, on the right-hand side, the beginning of a range
of flat-topped limestone hills. About a mile out of
Gargrave I came to the cross-roads where I must turn
left for Settle. The opposite arm of the signpost was
marked Kettlewell, but with no indication of distance. I reflected that if the name appeared on a
signpost, it was unlikely to be more than fifteen miles
away, and if we had done the seventeen miles from
Huntsham to Glastonbury in an afternoon march with
a pack-horse in hot weather, I could do the odd
fifteen miles to Kettlewell with one horse on a cool
day, especially as I had lunched earlier and had more
time to spare. Of course, I had no map beyond
Hetton ; but in hill country there are fewer roads
to lose your way among, and if I booked a room by
telephone there need be no forced march. The
beauty of the day had gone, and it would obviously
rain in an hour or so ; but I decided to risk it and,
turning my back on Settle, trotted along a quiet road
that ran parallel to the limestone hills. Not long
after I overtook a flock of sheep I had seen in Gargrave,
with a couple of shepherds and three or four dogs.
The rams were lamer than ever, and the men spoke
gloomily about the weather, and even more gloomily
about the slump in sheep. I pitied them for their

present job, for I have had bitter personal experience of driving sheep on modern roads. They said it was fourteen miles to Kettlewell, so I threaded my way through the flock and trotted on.

At Hetton post-office I stopped and asked for the telephone. This request seemed to cause some surprise ; but an old man showed me the instrument, which was kept in a separate part of the house, and I set to work on the directory list of Yorkshire hotels. The place I had heard of was not among them, so I tried another, and booked a room for myself and grazing for Ladybird. Having warned them that I might not come till late, I rode away with a pleasant sense of leisure and security.

As I had no map, I could only follow signposts, and found myself committed to a long and uninteresting stretch of busy road which, with more detailed knowledge, I might have been able to avoid. Before very long I saw a big lime-works ahead — considerably bigger than those near Buxton — and as far as I could make out, the road went straight through the middle of it. There seemed to be no way of circumventing the horror, nor had I any time to make a long circuit. The buildings and machinery were snow-white, and flanked the road on both sides for about 150 yards. The noise also was terrifying, and I could not blame Ladybird when she stopped dead and began to snort in alarm. I dismounted and coaxed her on a few steps. But further than

that she would not go of her own free will, so I
tried backing her, as I had done in Glossop. But
it is not easy to back a horse in traffic, and every
twenty yards or so I had to stop and soothe her
frayed nerves, for she was now sweating and trembling
with fear. So we progressed, backing and halting,
backing and halting, curiously watched by workmen
and by the drivers of passing cars. It took a long time
to do it, and when at last we got clear I gave Ladybird
a spell of rest and grazing at the roadside, while I sat
down beside her and ate some chocolate.

Near this spot was a left turning with a signpost
to Kettlewell. It was nearly five o'clock, and I had
another nine miles to go. The rain, which had been
threatening all afternoon, now began in earnest, and
before long I had to struggle into my mackintosh.
But the last six miles of that ride lay through the
beautiful country of upper Wharfedale ; and as the
clouds were high, and the rain of that widely spaced
variety which does not blot out distant objects altogether, I was not prevented from enjoying the
scenery. The flat rich valley with its brilliant green
grass and pleasant farms was bordered by steep, flat-
topped limestone hills, which here and there broke
into jutting crags and fantastic escarpments. The
road was narrow and fenced with drystone walls without much verge, so that the passing of the bright-red
Skipton bus was not without adventure.

By the time I reached Kettlewell, which stands

on the point where the valley turns west and narrows towards Buckden, it was raining hard, and all that night it poured in torrents, making me thankful to be under a roof. I entered the place too late for the usual salvo of 6 o'clock news. It had been a curious experience, night after night, to ride through a strange village, and everywhere hear the booming of the same cultured voice : " Further outlook unsettled. . . . At a meeting of the Cabinet. . . . Leeds United, nil. Billiards . . ." We may regard the people in the next dale as strangers, perhaps enemies ; but we all listen to (or, more correctly, allow ourselves to be addressed by) the same man saying the same thing at the same time. Does it make any difference, I wonder ? Perhaps not very much.

I went to the inn and found that Ladybird could be received at a farm across the bridge. The men were out and the womenfolk knew nothing about it. There was no stable, and the only building appeared to be a brand-new cowhouse with a concrete floor on which no cow had as yet set foot. This was jealously guarded, and I had to unsaddle in the rain, and give Ladybird her feed in the driest corner of the field.

The inn was well-appointed and charmingly furnished, and when in my shabby breeches I sat down to a four-course dinner with coffee in the lounge, I felt rather out of place, as my only worthy possession — saddle and bridle — were hidden away in a corner of the superfine cow-shed. Retiring early to my luxurious bed, I listened to the rain swishing down, and decided that if the weather were not better in the morning, I would take my week-end rest and stay another night. I read a few pages of *The Worst Journey* and fell asleep.

(4) *Saturday, Oct. 1 — Kettlewell to Hawes*

After a night's rain the weather improved. The wind had veered, and with a clearing sky and rising barometer, it seemed wiser to push on to Hawes. The inn was rather expensive, and in any case the season was advanced, and I must reach the Border by the following Friday at latest. Before fetching Ladybird, I hunted round the village for a fresh supply of corn. There was so much grass round Kettlewell that none of the farmers appeared to have either oats or bran. At last I found a carrier who kept a pony on dry feed, and he was willing to sell a small quantity of mixed oats and chaff. This did not much appeal to Ladybird, but it was the best I could get, and she had to make it do. Her coat was beginning to thicken for winter and, matted as it was by the heavy rain, she looked anything but smart, and was too damp for satisfactory grooming.

Then followed the easiest and pleasantest march of the whole trek. The motor road from Kettlewell to Hawes is by easy gradients and rather long ; but the hill route by Hubberholme and Oughtershaw is not more than seventeen miles, and from the top of the pass gives the most beautiful views on either side. Leaving Kettlewell, we trotted gaily along a level and quiet road to Buckden. Here I stopped at a shop and bought chocolate and a newspaper. There was plenty of time to spare, and I let Ladybird graze on the village green while I read *The Times*. Beyond Buckden the valley narrowed, and our road followed the river, which, swollen by a night's rain, was pouring noisily over the smooth limestone ledges. We rode through Hubberholme, with its ancient church and isolated hill farms. We were now in sheep country, and at points where the road was unfenced I saw notices warning motorists to beware of sheep. Presently I came to a farm-house which might, for all I knew, be the last inhabited place on this side of the summit. It was now just after twelve, and I might do well to get some lunch while I had the opportunity. I knocked, and asked for a glass of milk and a plate of bread-and-butter. I was shown into a chilly parlour, and in due course the milk and bread-and-butter were brought in, with cheese and a home-made cake as well. I hitched Ladybird to the railings, for it would be better to postpone her rest and feed till we reached the summit.

I rode on at a leisurely pace, enjoying the scene. It was one of those fresh days after rain that seem made for the wild. The sky was full of bright rolling clouds whose shadows chased each other on the hills. The river came down in a series of even, step-like little falls, which are characteristic of limestone country. There was no one about, and I was free to watch the play of light and shade, and listen to the murmur of running water, the call of ewe to lamb, and the beat of Ladybird's hoofs on the stony road. Soon we reached the hamlet of Oughtershaw, which rather surprisingly contains some kind of memorial hall, and a stone cross commemorating Queen Victoria's Jubilee. This monument was so worn and weathered by Yorkshire storms that it might have been set up by the first Christian missionaries. A little way above the village was a fold, closely packed with Swaledale sheep. There was no one in sight, but the flock had no doubt been gathered for the culling of draft ewes, and the shepherds had gone to dinner before beginning their work. Wishing to photograph the sheep, I prepared to give Ladybird her feed : with any luck the shepherds would be back before she finished. I removed her saddle and bridle, and shook out some of the Kettlewell mixture on my waterproof. She sniffed, blew contemptuously on it, and turned to the wayside grass. I climbed on the wall of the fold, and, while the astonished flock obligingly turned their horned faces to the camera, pressed the release piston.

Two young men with a dog appeared from the village, and after some talk they went into the fold

and started catching and sorting ewes. The fold was
too large for the flock, and the dog incompetent, and
seeing that they had difficulty in getting the sheep
packed closely enough for catching, I went in and
gave them a hand. Ladybird was left to her own
devices on the roadside, but as she never strayed far,
and was well in sight from the fold, I did not worry
about her. After the rain and the trampling (for
nothing makes a worse mess than folded sheep) the
place was a sea of sticky mud, and the sheep flew
round with all the agility of their mountain breed.
After a while the brothers decided to take them
back to the farm, where they could be confined in a
narrower space ; and catching Ladybird, I continued
my journey.

The name of Oughtershaw attracted me : it re-
called Auchterarder and Achterneed in Scotland, and
Oughterard in Galway. In the course of our journey
we had passed a number of villages whose names —
curious and amusing rather than beautiful — remain
in one's mind : Altarnun and Ashbrittle ; Dulcote
and Dinder ; Dordon and Didmarton ; Tetbury and
Tutbury ; Melmerby, Maxstoke, and Mytholmroyd ;
Hetton and Hatton ; Hubberholme, Gargrave, and
Slaggyford. A fine collection of unhackneyed sur-
names for the use of timid novelists afraid of being
prosecuted for libel.

The climb to the summit was not very stiff, and
there were beautiful views in all directions. To the

north lay the wide valley of Hawes, and westward a long empty glen wound upwards to a ridge, beyond which rose the flat-topped mass of Ingleborough. And this road, not being intended for motor traffic, was free from the black-and-white posts with glassy red Cyclops eyes which upon unfenced highways guide the traveller by night.

The descent was much steeper, and as it was a fine Saturday afternoon, we met two or three family cars labouring up in bottom gear, for picnics or a view.

After an easy and pleasant march, which was more like a riding tour than a journey, we reached Hawes in very good time. This little town, which is the agricultural centre of an extensive fell country, has no special interest for the casual visitor. But, as it happened, this was the day of one of the most important sheep sales of the year, and the place was crammed with farmers and dealers. Business was now over, but many people had stayed for the amusement fair that was in progress just outside the town. The inn which had been recommended by my hostess at Kettlewell was full, but I got a room at another one next door. They seemed doubtful about Lady-bird, but while we were talking, a man detached himself from the crowd and said that the butcher opposite, who was a friend of his, had suitable grazing. The butcher made no difficulties, and we went in search of the field, which was some distance from the inn and next to the fair ground. This did not please me much, as there were gipsies about, and Ladybird, who was unknown in the district and readily caught, might easily tempt a horse thief. My new friend, thinking that I objected to the field because the music might disturb the mare's slumbers, assured me that it was only a country fair, and would be over at eleven. So I decided to risk it, and we unsaddled in the field and carried the gear back to the hotel. My new friend offered to get me corn. While he was gone, I made discreet enquiries about him. I need not have bothered. In the morning he appeared with the corn and had Ladybird fed, groomed, saddled, and ready for the road. Before the shops closed, I went out and bought a new Ordnance sheet which I studied in front of the sitting-room fire. With any luck I should reach the Border in another four marching days, and as Ladybird and I were both quite fresh, I resolved to push on without taking a Sunday rest. Since abandoning the bedding at Cragg Vale we had been able to do a certain amount of trotting, which had shortened the time spent on the road — a good thing, for to-night the clocks would be put back, and we should have an hour less of daylight in the evening. My route for the next day was by Keld and Tan Hill to Brough. From here the easiest and shortest way to Scotland is by Appleby and Brampton to Gretna, but as the travelling is mostly on main roads and the scenery comparatively dull, I preferred to make for Alston and Haltwhistle, and cross the Border at Carter Bar. I wrote to the station-master at Carlisle, asking for a horse-box to be sent on Friday to whatever Scottish station was nearest to Carter Bar. I did not then know that all this district was served by the L.N.E.R.

The rector of our parish in Cornwall was motoring to Scotland by way of Gretna, and expected to cross my line of march somewhere between Bowes and Appleby. He wanted to see the lone horsewoman, and I wired him details of my proposed route, though in all that stretch of country there was but little chance of meeting.

The night was fine and clear, but the wind had begun to back south, and I did not feel very cheerful about to-morrow's weather. Had I known how wild it was to be, I might have stayed over the week-end in Hawes, but having no friends and nothing to do in the place, it was better to push on. The solitary woman traveller who frequents inns is at a great disadvantage. Excluded from the freemasonry of bar or commercial room, she must wilt in some musty parlour, where has been no fire for six months and no air since Creation. No drinks, no talk, no company ; only a cracked piano and a few artificial flowers. Such is the price of supposed dignity and virtue !

X

Westmoreland and Cumberland

(1) *Sunday, Oct. 2 — Hawes to Brough*

MORNING came with a strong south wind and ragged
flying clouds. It was not raining yet, but soon would
be, and my intimate knowledge of mountain weather
told me that we were in for a thoroughly bad day.
This was a pity, for the scenery promised to be as good
as the day before, if not better. How I longed for the
fine days wasted on many a dull Midland march!

Leaving the town, we turned northwards, crossed
the river and railway, and began to climb into the
hills. The wind was rising, and the clouds dropped
lower on the southern ramparts of the valley. The
top of the Kettlewell pass had disappeared, and a
thick curtain of rain was sweeping down the glen,
where yesterday we had ridden in sunshine. We
had been travelling about forty minutes when the
first drops reached us, and in a few moments the
world was lost in vapour. Seeing that this would
be no passing shower, I dismounted and pulled on
my mackintosh trousers. They were made for a tall
man, but I turned up the hems, thus providing a gutter

to protect my shoes. At intervals I stopped to let out the accumulated water.

We climbed steadily. The wild narrow glen was empty of life, and the upper slopes of the hills invisible. Before long we passed a group of small pot-holes known as the Butter-tubs. These were the only specimens of limestone caves and holes I saw on the march, for most of these are in the Ingleborough district, which lay well to the west of my route. At the top of the pass, where the road descends towards Thwaite, was a closed gate. A man sprang out of the mist to open it. He must have been waiting there on the rather remote chance of a passing car. On such a stormy Sunday morning so late in the year, travellers were surely scarce. I doubt if I met four motors all day. Just short of Thwaite I turned left and followed a lateral valley towards Keld.

It was now blowing hard, and we took our mid-morning rest at the gable-end of a solid stone-built cattle-house. In this country of small hill farms the buildings are not all beside the homestead, but dispersed through the fields for convenience of feeding and shelter. The rain was fine and dense, and fell from low trailing clouds, which obscured everything at a distance, but now and then, livid pewter-like gleams would fall upon the landscape, with the shifting play of light that gives to even the wettest day in the mountains its own peculiar charm. Before very long we passed Cat Hole Inn. Here we were in the wild upper stretches of Swaledale. The river, swollen with rain, brawled noisily over its limestone ledges, and below the inn, plunged into a rocky thickly-wooded gorge — a tempting place to explore, had one the time and the weather. Crossing an ancient bridge, we turned right and climbed out of the valley by a series of sharp zigzags. At the top was an apparently limitless expanse of soaking moor across which the road was looped like a strip of dirty tape, with its end lost in the vapours of the near horizon. The wind had risen to gale force, but it blew from behind, and on this comparatively level plateau we were able to make good speed. My tweed hat was a sponge, and so was the sheep-skin in any place uncovered by my body. Water streamed from coat and trousers into the turned-up hems, which needed frequent emptying. But as an ex-moor farmer I had been out on days much worse than this, and did not very much care. In the middle of this wind-swept wilderness, with no house in sight, I was surprised to see a flock of sixteen geese contentedly grazing.

Soon after one o'clock I came in sight of the lonely inn at Tan Hill, which at 1735 feet claims to be the highest public-house in England. It was a plain whitewashed building with a large porch and beside it some ruinous outhouses, in which I hoped to find shelter for Ladybird while I had lunch. I knocked at the door. The astonished landlord took me to a shed which had once been a stable, but was now used to house goats. The goat in possession was tied up, and with much coaxing we induced Ladybird to enter. It took me some time to unsaddle, for the prolonged wet and cold had made my wrists weak and fingers stiff, so that the girth straps and bridle buckles gave me much trouble. I rubbed down the mare with a sack, gave her a liberal feed, and returned to the house in quest of food. Having shed my dripping coat and trousers in the porch, I walked into the main room, where four black-clad and serious-looking men were sitting round a blazing fire. There was a large table in the window, but the landlord's daughter insisted on serving my eggs and tea in a prim and vault-like parlour, which she warmed by lighting a large table lamp.

A plague on all this respectability. The rout of Bacchus round the fire was surely the most unconvivial crowd that ever gathered in a licensed house. I gobbled my food and came out of the parlour with my dripping hat in my hand, and on the pretext of drying it, took a seat by the fire. This unladylike conduct shocked the landlord's daughter, but I toasted myself in peace and comfort, and soon had complete control of the conversation. The gentlemen, who looked like a benchful of Quaker elders, had come out from Bradford on a Sunday spree, thus justifying the Continental legend of the Englishman who takes his pleasures sadly.

My Kingdom for a Horse

The weather was getting worse. Tearing myself away from the fire, I went to the shed for Ladybird. She was now fairly dry, but had left the whole of her corn, probably in suspicion of a strange stable. From Tan Hill our route lay north-west towards Brough. The wind was veering more westerly, and blew across and slightly against us. The first two miles were unspeakable. The road was unfenced ; there was no shelter anywhere, and in October, at nearly 2000 feet above sea-level, the air in a gale of wind is cold. The rain drove in merciless horizontal shafts, and I had difficulty in making Ladybird face it. But after a while we came into a region of enclosed moorland where the road was bordered by solid stone walls, which were high enough to protect the horse and the lower part of the rider's body. The relief of reaching such shelter can be realised only by experience. We began the long descent ; but as the slope faced west we gained little from it in actual protection. It was still pouring, but the clouds were higher and the rain less fine, so that it was possible to see for a considerable distance. Even in such weather the views were magnificent. The fells dropped abruptly to the rolling, well-wooded plain of Appleby, beyond which, half seen in cloud, rose the mountains of the Lake District.

We descended rapidly to Barras station, where a side road branches north-east to Barnard Castle. Below Barras our course was straight and level to

Brough. A few draggled cyclists overtook us, and we met a number of people with umbrellas perilously open, who were struggling home from afternoon chapel. We were now back in civilisation, and also out of Yorkshire, the first county I had crossed alone. Brough Castle was in sight, and the next thing was to find a night's lodging, for the end of Summer Time makes a serious difference to the traveller. A big herd of Shorthorns was coming out of a field, driven by a friendly-looking farmer. I asked him if he knew of grazing for Ladybird, and he offered hospitality not only to the mare but to her rider as well. Needless to say I was delighted to find so easy an ending to a hard day. His farm was near the Castle, and from this outlying field it was a good half-mile to the homestead.

My host was not only a farmer but a big dealer, who travelled over an extensive district to buy sheep and cattle, and visited most of the north-western markets from Crewe to Carlisle. His wife and family gave me a great welcome, with the usual north-country profusion of food. The people of Westmoreland and Cumberland are as hospitable as those of Yorkshire, and have as a rule more outward courtesy and charm of manner. As it was Sunday, and the farm well-served with labour, everyone in the house had plenty of leisure, and we must have spent five or six hours in agricultural talk, broken by a large tea and an even larger supper.

My Kingdom for a Horse

My host knew the fell country in and out. As a dealer he had visited remote hill farms in search of lambs and store cattle, and saw places where men and things remained as they had been a hundred years ago. He told me a tale of two bachelor brothers who farmed a few acres in some isolated dale. The younger one was very lazy, and his brother had much trouble in getting him to do his share of the work. He even refused to help lift the potatoes. So the older man went out to the field, and after digging for a time, took a half-crown from his pocket, rubbed it on the ground till it was well coated with earth, and replaced it. Later, when they were sitting at dinner, he showed the coin to his brother. " I found it in the potato plot," he added casually. That afternoon the whole crop was lifted by the sluggard, but no hoard of coins rewarded his labours.

I heard many complaints of sheep killed by motorists and of thefts by lorry drivers, who, when hired to take a large batch of sheep to the railway or to market, would abstract one or two from each load, and allege a mistake in checking the number. Wholesale raids on mountain flocks by thieves operating at night with lorries are becoming alarmingly common, and it is most difficult for farmers and shepherds to guard against them.

In these days the farmers of Brough get coal by rail, like everyone else. But formerly they thought nothing of sending carts ten miles into the fells, where, at an altitude of nearly 2000 feet, was an outcrop of coal. The quality was not very good, but it could be had for the labour of carting it home. I remembered noticing some disused workings near Tan Hill, but supposed them to be the remains of a lead mine of which I had been told. But this, it seems, was the place. A long trail with a coal-laden cart !

The night was very wild. A westerly gale screamed through the trees, with frequent pelts of rain or hail. After some hesitation we had turned out Ladybird, for there was plenty of grass in the field, and plenty of cover. But through the night, as I lay in my warm bed, I thought of her standing tail to wind in the lee of some hedge, and pitied her. But she always hated a stable, and with the company of my host's horses I think she was content.

(2) *Monday, Oct. 3 — Brough to Melmerby*

I was now once more without a map, but the limited choice of roads made it of little importance. My next objective was Alston, where I expected to find letters, and from there I hoped to ride by Haltwhistle to Carter Bar. My host advised me to go to Alston by Hilton and Melmerby, rather than to follow the longer motor road by Middleton-in-Teesdale. The distance from Brough to Alston was about thirty miles, and Melmerby would make a good halting-place for the night. The only trouble was that the Rector, knowing that I should be somewhere between Brough and Alston, would be looking for me at some point on the obvious Middleton road. But I must risk that. And it was well that I did, for, as I heard a few days later, the war scare had prevented him from starting at all.

The first hour's travel was a rather dull grind along the main road to Appleby. I had always wanted to visit this town, for in the palmy days of railway travel hardly anyone in the South had seen it, and most of us did not even know anybody who had been there. Appleby was a mere name in a geography book, the county town of Westmoreland, and we had less knowledge of it than of Lhasa or La Paz. But now with the advent of motors, Appleby has come into its own. It is a stage on the western route to Scotland, and had I not wished to avoid main roads, I should have made its acquaintance. But my nearest point was six miles distant, and now I shall probably die without knowing more about Appleby than I did thirty years ago.

Three miles out of Brough I turned right, and followed a delightful grass track to Hilton. This track, and in fact the whole road from Brough to Melmerby, hugged the western side of the great central block of fells that stretched unbroken to the Border. The lower slopes were in cultivation, and dotted with trim-looking upland farms, with good

Shorthorn cattle and sheep, mostly Swaledales, that summered on the hills. Away to the west, far beyond Appleby, was the rampart of the Lakeland hills, falling away in the north-west to the plain of Carlisle and the Solway shore. Behind were the fells of the North Riding, dominated by table - topped Ingleborough. A memorable view, and the fresh bright day, with flying clouds and gleams of sun, only increased its beauty. But there was more rain on the way ; the wind was backing south, and from Lancashire a dirty film of cloud was rising, which before long would drain the sky of its brightness.

We rode gaily on the turf track, sometimes trotting, sometimes cantering, so that the bananas I carried were squashed to a pulp. Traces of the wet summer and late harvest were everywhere visible. Some hay was still out in tramp-cocks, and there was much corn in the stook. In one place I saw a field of seeds and another of oats still uncut. Little white-washed farms were strung upon the road, and clustered here and there into hamlets, like the beads of an irregular prehistoric necklace. At one point a pair of Clydesdale horses came out of an open gate and followed us for some distance, circling round Lady-bird with clumsy gambols.

Beyond Hilton the road curved away from the fells ; the farms were larger, and the Swaledales were replaced by Border Leicesters, many of them dyed a delicate saffron colour. It was here, in the midst of all this pastoral peace, that Ladybird got her worst fright. In one of the roadside fields was a shooting party out after partridges. One of the men rose suddenly behind the hedge, causing the mare to jump almost out of her skin. A little further on we passed a halted gipsy cart with a piebald colt tethered behind it, and this unexpected and I suppose sinister apparition had much the same effect as the lime-works near Kettlewell. She stopped dead, and had to be coaxed past the terror. Then we saw a late foal, no doubt born in August, and in another field a strange collection of birds — some hundreds of rooks feeding with a flock of geese and a dozen hens.

I had lunch at a wayside inn. The landlord took me to a little grass plot up the road where he kept a few hens. There was not much grazing for Ladybird, but I had plenty of corn in my bag, so we had to make that do. The innkeeper had been a farmer, and was the only person I met on my travels who seemed to want war. His wife could give me nothing but boiled eggs and tea, but as there were no men about, I was allowed to eat it by the fire in the bar parlour, which made up for all deficiencies.

I came out to find the sky completely overcast. The wind was rising, and Skiddaw, Helvellyn, and Ingleborough were lost in the advancing rain. To save dismounting later, I unstrapped my waterproof and mackintosh trousers, and made all preparations for another soaking ride. And I got it. Luckily the

wind was behind us, and it was this mercy that made
tolerable the last few days of my ride. Had I been
forced to fight my way south against the incessant
gales and driving rain there would have been something to complain about. As it was I turned up my
collar, pulled down my hat and ran north before
the storm.

Before long the road curved back to the fells,
and we reached Melmerby about four o'clock. The
road was empty, the country drowned in rain, and
I saw nothing to remember or record. Melmerby, a
good-sized village with a green, had several public-
houses. I was advised to try the Shepherd Inn, where
they had good grazing and a stable. The stable proved
to be a large and handsome barn with big double
doors opening on the village street. But it was fairly
empty, and I found a hook for hitching up the mare,
a pail to feed her in, and a sack with which to rub
her down. As usual she was in a hurry to get outside,
and after tea I took her to the field, and got drenched
in the process, though it was quite near at hand.

A ham-and-egg tea was spread in the sitting-room,
where the old-world musty smell peculiar to little-
used country parlours was being driven out by a
roaring fire. There was no one in the inn, and I had
the best bedroom. I also had a superb bath in an
unexpected and brand-new bathroom — so new that
the linoleum had not yet been laid. The large lofty
room was painted with shining white enamel, and in

the midst was a modern rectangular bath. The keepers of country inns and boarding-houses have suddenly realised that without modern plumbing they are lost. Would that they might consider the possibility, for breakfast, lunch, high tea or supper, of some alternative to eggs and bacon!

But it was churlish to complain. Warmed by my wallow in the modern bath, and fortified by ham and eggs, I drew a broken-springed armchair to the fire, wrote up my diary, and read a chapter or two of *The Worst Journey*. Then I began to feel bored. An uneventful ride of twenty miles is not physically tiring, and when the shortening days compel you to seek an early halt, you will find yourself washed and fed by seven o'clock, but not yet ready for sleep. And if the night is dark and wet, and you are the only person in a strange inn, you may be a little dull. This is one of the many arguments for summer travel.

(3) *Tuesday, Oct. 4 — Melmerby to Hallbankgate*

This was the day of a memorable storm that swept Britain from end to end, and was perhaps the worst I have ever encountered out of doors. It had been raining and blowing all night, and the dawn-light struggled feebly through a whirl of ragged dingy clouds that raced before an ever-increasing gale. I found Ladybird cowering miserably under a lee hedge, and resolved that somehow or other she should spend her next night under cover. As we plodded dismally out of Melmerby, rain was still falling, but the wind was too high for a heavy downpour.

Alston is said to be the highest market-town in England. I cannot vouch for the truth of this, but I do know that it lies in a cup of the hills, and on every side but one must be approached by high and exposed passes. My road wound up the western face of the fell-rampart which we had skirted the whole of the previous day. From bottom to top it was raked by the blast. There was no shelter of any kind on the wind-ward side, for the road was fenced with wire, with here and there a strip of low ragged thorn hedge. We slogged up. The wind tore at us, and in its heaviest gusts appeared to pin us to the face of the hill. It screeched madly through the wires of the fence and the lean tortured branches of thorns. In one or two places lower down were clumps of skinny pines, or a strip of thicker and better-grown thorns, which offered a momentary shelter. We crawled from one to another, halting in the lee of each to gather breath. A lorry clattered past, loaded with stone, but its noise was lost in the general uproar. At each spot of shelter Ladybird wished to stop and turn her tail to the blast, so that I had much trouble in urging her forward. On a clear day we should have had an uninterrupted view of the Lake mountains, but now there was nothing but a welter of clouds and whirling vapour and driving scuds of rain.

My Kingdom for a Horse

The final zigzags, where all shelter ceased, were fearful. I was lucky to know the direction, for the signpost at the top had worked loose, and its arms were waving in aimless circles, showing Alston at every point of the compass in turn. Not far beyond the signpost was a wooden bungalow, which proved to be a R.A.C. tea-room. We crawled under its lee, and as we stood to rest, I flattened my nose against the dusty pane. Within were wicker chairs and little tables, all neatly stacked for the winter, and the place had the forsaken, unseemly look of summer's pleasure at the wild back-end of the year. The shriek of the storm was truly fearful, and I should not have been surprised if our flimsy refuge had been lifted into the air and whirled away to the North Sea.

I waited a few minutes and then led forth the unwilling Ladybird. But, once in the open, she was so eager to fly before the gale that she would hardly stand for me to mount. For the moment our troubles were over. Our course lay east and downhill ; the road descended in easy gradients, and we were soon well below the summit, trotting gaily down to Alston. We had a halt for grazing half-way down, and did the whole ten miles from Melmerby in just under two hours.

The little town, with its grey houses set in a circle of wild rain-soaked fells, had a grim forbidding look. The river in spate rolled under the bridge in yeasty tumult. The gale roared in the trees and snatched at the clothes of people on the road. I had business in the town, and wanted to leave Ladybird under cover. But I could hear of no inn with a stable, so the only thing was to find a farm on the road to the north. The first place I tried was in the hands of caretakers, who would not give grazing without the permission of their employer. Then I saw a small private house with a paddock behind. There was no stable, but I was offered the use of the field. This was less sheltered than I could have wished, but it was getting late, and there seemed no other choice. Leaving Ladybird, I returned to the town, went up to the post-office, and asked for letters. There were none.

This was a blow. The letter from the station-master at Carlisle should have been there, with information about the horse-box. And unless the box were ordered now, I might not get it in time. I must go to the little station at Alston and make further enquiries, and also must somehow or other get hold of a map. On my way up to the post-office I had noticed a building called a Literary Institute ; perhaps it might contain a library or a reading-room with local maps. I went in. The place was crowded with people who were busy with preparations for a sale of work. Seeing a man in clerical dress who was no doubt in authority, I asked if there were any maps in the Institute. He thought not, but kindly offered to show me his own. We went to the Vicarage, where he spread out the relevant Ordnance sheets. If I still wished to go by Carter Bar, the most suitable station for entrainment would be Riccarton Junction, and the best way to it was by Haltwhistle, Haydon Bridge, Bellingham, and Falstone. But it was a long road, and over wild and exposed country. The weather had broken, and we were in for an indefinite period of wind and rain. It might be better to take the shorter and lower route. The obvious way was by Brampton to Gretna ; but a quieter and pleasanter ride could be had by crossing the Border north of Longtown and entraining at Langholm.

Leaving the Vicarage, I went down to the station and ordered a horsebox to be ready at Langholm on Friday, October 7. On my way back I bought some corn and looked about for a place for lunch. My memories of Alston food are not pleasant, for I had the worst and dearest meal of the whole journey. While I waited for it to come, I began to wonder where I should spend the night. Brampton was the obvious place, but it is nineteen miles from Alston, and we should not get clear of the town before 1.30 at the earliest. Also, having already marched ten miles under stiff conditions, we were not fresh. The road to Brampton, though it did not cross any high hills, ran north-west, so that we should no longer have a favourable wind. There was a commercial traveller at the next table, and I asked him if he knew of any place between Alston and Brampton where I could get a night's lodging. The reply was not encouraging. There were three or four villages, but almost certainly without accommodation for travellers except perhaps Hallbankgate, where there was said to be a temperance inn. This place was only four miles short of Brampton, but the saving of four miles at the end of a long march is a great thing, and might allow us to arrive before dark. The traveller envied me my horse, but at that moment I would not have been sorry for the loan of his car.

I returned to the paddock where I had left Lady-bird. She was huddled under the lee of a very inadequate hedge, and gave me a reproachful look, though I fancy that she had chosen this refuge less for its problematical shelter than for the sake of another horse on the further side. I saddled up and turned towards Brampton. The wind came either from the side or against us, according to the bends of the road. Although the valley in which we were riding was, compared with the hill-tops, a sheltered glade, the roar of the storm effectively drowned the noise of overtaking traffic, and whenever we met its full force, blew us to a standstill. Streams shouted in spate, but I could not hear them, and the laboured uphill panting of a goods train must be inferred from the sharp forced jets of steam which the wind snatched and whirled into space.

In Slaggyford, the first village, I called at the post-office. The horse-box was going to cost more than

My Kingdom for a Horse

I had expected, and I wired for more money to be sent to Langholm. The postmistress thought that there was a temperance inn at Hallbankgate, but no other village on this side of Brampton would be likely to have accommodation for travellers. So Hallbankgate it must be. Brampton was out of the question : the day was too short, the distance too great, and Ladybird already showing signs of stiffness and fatigue. Even Hallbankgate was a full ten miles away, and unless we could make good speed, there was no hope of getting there before dark.

We plodded on, and soon passed the turn to Haltwhistle, not without much regret, for I had set my heart on entering Scotland by Carter Bar. But the shorter route was a wise choice, for the weather did not mend, and soon after this Ladybird showed signs of incipient lameness. So far we had not been much troubled with rain. But later in the afternoon the wind began to moderate, and there were frequent showers of rain and hail, with brief intervals of sunshine. Near Lambley we encountered a fierce black squall, which swooped suddenly down from the hills, devouring the daylight. Hailstones leapt on the road and rattled harshly on iron roofs. From the lee of a cottage gable we watched the storm sweep by, scattering cyclists and driving flocks to shelter. To the north-west, beyond the moving curtains of hail, I could see wild gleams of sun on the solitary fells that lies between Hadrian's Wall and the Border.

Westmoreland and Cumberland

The squall passed eastward with a sheen of broken rainbow arches and the glitter of millions of raindrops under the westering sun. I saw banks and towers of glowing cumulus piled on a cliff-like escarpment of distant fells, and the wide horizons of this empty world made me long to turn back there. But when we emerged from the shelter of the gable, Ladybird was going definitely lame, and I made the rest of the day's journey on foot. Since leaving the pack-horse, we had done several long marches on hard roads, and I blamed myself for having made the bad weather an excuse for pushing on at too fast a pace.

At Midgholme there was no inn, and nothing like a farm. The villages we were passing had the air of settlements once industrial, but now driven by hard times to the practice of half-hearted and unprofitable husbandry. On the left of the road was a forbidding line of hills, and on the right a stretch of barren semi-cultivated country, with here and there a casual slag-heap or meaningless bit of machinery, which reminded me of derelict mining districts in Cornwall. At Tindale I saw a disused smelting works with rows of grim-looking cottages, but again no inn and no farm near the road. The sun was setting in wild splendour, casting a stormy blood-red glare on wet slates and shining tarmac. I felt weary and depressed. The people I met seemed dour and uncommunicative, and passed without interest or gaiety. It was still some distance to Hallbankgate, and I began to wonder

if the temperance inn existed, and even if it did,
whether they would take me in. Had I known that
there would be no mail waiting at Alston, I could
have gone direct from Melmerby to Brampton, thus
saving several miles.

The last two miles to Hallbankgate were covered
in the dark. On reaching the village I enquired for
a farm, and was lucky to find one close at hand, where
Ladybird was given a warm stable and a good feed.
I arranged for her to be left in all night with hay in
the rack. Then I went in search of the temperance
inn. It was as I feared. Nothing would persuade
them to give me a bed. The landlady, unmoved by
tales of long marches in wind and rain, of dark nights
and lame horses, merely repeated in a dreary mono-
tone, " It is not convenient ". So I went back to
consult the farmer's wife. She advised me to try
the caretaker of the reading-room, who was believed
once to have taken a lodger. With some difficulty I
found the reading-room, but the caretaker's wing was
closed and unlighted. I climbed the stairs, broke in
on an astonished and rather glum crowd of villagers
playing billiards, and learnt from them that the caretaker had gone to an evening class and would not be
back till bedtime. Once more I returned to the
farm, and was taken to three or four cottages, but
none of the inhabitants felt inclined to accommodate
a stranger.

There was nothing for it but to leave Ladybird at

the farm, and push on myself to Brampton — a sad waste of energy, for I should have to come back for the mare in the morning. By a stroke of luck — the only one in all that wretched day — a bus was leaving for Brampton in a few minutes. Half an hour later I stood in a comfortable bedroom in the best hotel, tired, wet, hungry, but within a day's march of the Border.

(4) *Wednesday, Oct. 5 — Hallbankgate to Longtown*

Next day, in consideration of the weather and Ladybird's lameness, I decided on a short march of fifteen miles to Longtown. While enjoying an opulent breakfast at the Brampton hotel, I had some conversation with a commercial traveller at the next table. He was bemoaning the stormy autumn and the rigours of travelling by car from Newcastle to Carlisle. This road is very exposed, and driving from east to west, he would have met the full force of the gale. But when I told him that I had encountered the same storm on horseback on the Alston fells, his eyes nearly dropped out of his head. So relative are our ideas of comfort and of weather.

I caught a bus in the market-place and returned to Hallbankgate, where I found Ladybird groomed and saddled. She was walking much better, and as a few days' rest in Scotland left her completely sound in all paces, I concluded that her lameness was a temporary trouble, caused by hard roads and fatigue. The village looked less forbidding in daylight, and the kindness of the people at the farm did much to leave pleasant memories of one of our last halting-places.

The wind had moderated, but every few minutes we were assailed by drenching showers. They were so fierce that when I dismounted for a moment to adjust my mackintosh trousers, the sheep-skin was soaked and heavy as Gideon's fleece, and could be dried only by gradually squeezing out the water with the weight of my body. The four miles to Brampton seemed much longer than they had done in darkness on the bus, and we saw nothing of the smallest interest.

From Brampton to Longtown was a dull march of eleven miles along a straight, level, and featureless road. There were several beautiful old bridges, one of them over the Irthing, a river whose source is in that waste of moors on the Northumberland border which I had so much wanted to cross. Here we narrowly missed a collision with two lorries laden with straw. My enjoyment of bridges, which seem designed for idle loitering and meditation, was generally spoilt by the need for ceaseless watchfulness, for on major roads these bottle-necked passages are the worst place to meet heavy traffic. The country was fertile and slightly undulating. South-

westward it fell away to the plain of Carlisle, while
to the north and east it rose gradually to a long line
of distant fells, purple and brown in the play of light
and shade, and low enough to give an impression of
space and emptiness, which is the essence of the
Border country. The land was heavily stocked with
Shorthorn and Ayrshire cattle, and with Cheviot
sheep. Every farm was flanked with tidy rows of
cylindrical corn-stacks, and the solid outbuildings
were in striking contrast with the flimsy, ramshackle
barns and sheds of the more genial south.

Then came the usual problem — where to get
lunch. Villages were scarce along the road, and the
only possible place was Smithfield, which had an inn
of imposing appearance. But as so often at country
pubs, food was scarce and unwillingly produced.
The door was opened by an old man. He summoned
his sister, a thin, dry, withered crone, who with
much reluctance consented to give me tea, boiled
eggs, and cheese. I was ushered into an ice-cold
parlour which had obviously not been aired or fired
for months, and sat there shivering to wait for my
meagre repast. Ladybird had found more pleasing
quarters in a field of grass near by. The eggs had not
been laid recently, and the tea was weak, but thank
goodness ! hot. The cheese was of the emasculated,
cardboard-box variety and very dry. Parenthetically,
why is it so difficult to get an honest slice from a
whole cheese in an English public-house ? If this

mania for wrapping everything up continues, we shall soon have our children born in cellophane paper. I ate my dismal meal, every crumb of it, for I was very hungry, and the tea helped to restore a little warmth to my chilled bones ; but it was dear, and for the first time I was charged for Ladybird's midday grazing. So farewell, Smithfield. I leave without regret.

The wind was so cold that I walked the rest of the way to Longtown, which we reached soon after 3.30. On the southern outskirts of the town I noticed a pleasant-looking farm, where I arranged for Ladybird's grazing and stabling. Leaving her in charge of a friendly youth, I walked into the town, fixed up my own night quarters, and then went to the station to see if there was any news of my horsebox. I found that it had been ordered, and also discovered that Langholm was the terminus of a branch line from Riddings Junction. This station, though actually on the Border, was several miles nearer to Longtown, so that it would be easier and a little cheaper to entrain there. Had I known all this sooner, I might have pushed on to Riddings that night, and had the horsebox on Thursday instead of Friday. But it was too late for that now. I explored the resources of Longtown — it was, as usual, early closing day — until nightfall, and then had tea, and spent a quiet and rather dull evening alone in the hotel sitting-room.

(5) *Thursday, Oct. 6 — Longtown to Riddings Junction*

The next morning was unsettled but reasonably dry, and I rode the six miles to Riddings in comfort and at a leisurely pace. I could not believe that this was the last day of my journey, which had lasted nearly five weeks, and by this time seemed the normal condition of life. The road was very quiet, and ran for most of its length through woods. I met nothing of note save a man driving sheep, who asked if the mare was for sale.

Presently I turned left, and rode down a lane which ended at the white railings of a wayside station. Beyond it was the river Liddel, and on the further bank, Scotland. I hitched Ladybird to the fence, and went in search of the stationmaster. He was not busy, and we had a long talk. The horsebox would be ready on Friday afternoon, but the Edinburgh express, to which it was to be attached, did not stop at Riddings, so I must join it at Longtown, while the horsebox, for some reason best known to the railway company, would go down to Carlisle with the afternoon train and be hitched on there. There is no village at Riddings, only the station and a farm. I asked the stationmaster if he knew of any house where I could stay for the night. He thought that the farmer next door might put us up, and offered to take me across and introduce me personally.

At this farm I spent a very pleasant twenty-four hours. The farmer and his wife could not get over their astonishment that anyone coming from Cornwall should have landed in Riddings. The place is quiet enough, but not as quiet as my original destination, Riccarton Junction. This, according to the porter, who had once worked there, was a veritable hell on earth — no road, no houses near, and snowed-up half the year ! The farm-house was so near the line that it shook with the thunder of passing trains, and clocks were set by them. I spent some time exploring the farm and looking at stock, though the weather had turned stormy again, with fierce hail squalls, and thunder and lightning. In the afternoon I made an expedition to Langholm, where I ran into another early closing day, but was able to collect my letters and the money for the horsebox.

On Friday afternoon I packed the saddle and bridle in a sack, filled another bag with oats and hay for the journey, and led Ladybird into the station. The farmer came with me, and assisted by the station-master and porter, we coaxed the nervous pony into the box. The stalls were built for bigger horses, and the padding was rather too high, but she seemed quite comfortable and came out undamaged. She went down to Carlisle about an hour before I was due to start for Longtown, and as the train with horsebox attached went thundering past the windows of the farm-house, I was glad to think that the end of the trek was likely to be as quiet and unspectacular as the start from the yard at Newton.

In a Horsebox

THIRTY hours later I was sitting on the bench of the groom's compartment, looking at Ladybird through an open shutter, and feeding her with mouthfuls of hay. The train, an express goods, was jolting over the mountain track from Dingwall to Kyle of Lochalsh. The mare, who had been in terror for the first few hours, seemed now resigned to an eternity of railway travel, and was munching hay with obvious pleasure. We had had an exasperating journey — a semi-fast train to Edinburgh, a long wait ; a slow train to Perth, another wait ; a slow train to Inverness, a faster one to Dingwall ; and then a lightning change into the goods. It was bitterly cold in the horsebox, and the guard invited me to share his fire in the van as soon as he could get it going. But at Garve he came along the platform with a long face, and said, " It's nae use. I canna get sticks."

I arrived at Strathascaig as a thief in the night. I was not expected till the next train ; the Laird was at a sale in Dingwall, and had left a note of regret with the stationmaster, which for some reason I never received. The mare was unloaded with the help of a bystander, for the railway officials were absorbed in some other business, or perhaps asleep. I left my rucksack and saddlery for the Laird to bring up in his car, and led Ladybird along the familiar road to the farm, where I hitched her quietly in the stable, and to the astonishment of Herself, walked into the house as if I had never left it.

So I am home again. Achnabo is no more, but Strathascaig is unchanged, and as it seems, unchangeable. There are, of course, some minor innovations. The scythes, for want of skilled men, have been replaced with a one-horse mower, drawn by Tess, the large, placid Clydesdale mare. An iron gate has been brought from the riverside pasture to block the Cursing Gap. The old dogs are dead, and there is a new cat. The Laird has grown a little fatter, and Herself a little thinner. But the welcome is the same, and so is the rain. I must have brought it with me, for they say that all three years of my absence were very dry. There is no day fair enough to dip sheep or (luckily for me) to lift potatoes.

This penance I had hoped to escape, but two days before I left there was a blink of sun, and we went out to claw the slimy crop from the split furrows. A cold June and an abnormally wet autumn had spoilt the yield ; we bent low over the cold dank ground, covered with dying weeds and rotting shaws, and wearily threw the little earth-clogged tubers into the pails. It was all unchanged — the meditative plough-man, the long Gaelic conversations, the idle small boys, the distracted dogs, the passing train, the Laird fiddling with the string on the sacks. I only stayed an hour, for my back is stiff — too stiff for this job, anyhow. Next day I caught Ladybird and rode the four miles to Achnabo. The house was empty and the steading deserted. The fences were in good order, but rushes and bracken had invaded the empty fields. I cantered along the loch-side, and looked from afar on the shepherd's house, now occupied by a stranger. We had been gone nearly four years, and at that moment I did not wish to see the farm again.

Later I went to Morvern to help a sheep-farming friend with his belated hay-making. Every day the rain came down in sheets, and the hill was like a sponge. The hay was out in big tramp-coils, and thus fairly secure, but we longed to see it safe in the capacious barn, which extended over the whole length of byres and stables below. But Morvern is a wet land, and October 1938 was one of the rainiest months on record. The hay stayed out, and we fell to sawing wood to get an appetite for dinner and justify a long afternoon spent over the fire.

So I am back once more — and with great pleasure and relief. Not that the Highlands have escaped " improvement " — far from it, and the remoter the place, the greater and more startling the change. Twenty-five years ago the outlying districts, especially in the Islands, remained much as they were in the eighteenth century. Now, in the matter of health, education, housing, roads, the Hebridean crofter is better off than many workers in the South, whether in town or country. Well-built roads are everywhere being made, on which cars, lorries, and buses can ply. The old thatched houses have mostly been replaced with boxes of concrete or corrugated iron. Fishing-boats are fitted with motor engines, lone shielings have aerials lashed to the chimneys, crofters go about their work in dungarees and rubber boots, and young girls walk to church in the latest fashions from Glasgow. Modernisation has come with a rush, like a spring tide, submerging the ancient landmarks. But its effects are superficial. The people are the same, and the lasting things — hills, rivers, seas, and skies — remain dominant, with some quality of remoteness, at once restful and stimulating, which will resist the assault of all passing fashions.

For most of us the permanent family home is a thing of the past. Professional people live in flats and villas, following in semi-nomadic fashion the march of their work. Thus they have often no special attachment for the place where they were bred, and if they later seek a home, it will probably be in a land which appeals to some quality in themselves, a land which, in the haunting Latin phrase, smiles at them — *arridet eis*. And so, though an alien in the Highlands, I prefer to live there, and rejoice in my return.

NORTH UIST, *March* 1939

THE END

Printed in Great Britain by R. & R. CLARK, LIMITED, *Edinburgh*

SCOTLAND

Cumberland

Westmorland

Yorkshire

Derbyshire

Warwickshire

Gloucester

Somerset

Dorsetshire

Cornwall

Other titles in the Equestrian Travel Classic series published by The Long Riders' Guild Press. We are constantly adding to our collection, so for an up-to-date list please visit our website: **www.thelongridersguild.com**

Title	Author
Southern Cross to Pole Star – Tschiffely's Ride	Aime Tschiffley
Tale of Two Horses	Aime Tschiffley
Bridle Paths	Aime Tschiffely
This Way Southward	Aime Tschiffely
Bohemia Junction	Aime Tschiffely
Through Persia on a Sidesaddle	Ella C. Sykes
Through Russia on a Mustang	Thomas Stevens
Across Patagonia	Lady Florence Dixie
A Ride to Khiva	Frederick Burnaby
Ocean to Ocean on Horseback	Williard Glazier
Rural Rides – Volume One	William Cobbett
Rural Rides – Volume Two	William Cobbett
Adventures in Mexico	George F. Ruxton
Travels with A Donkey in the Cevennes	Robert Louis Stevenson
Winter Sketches from the Saddle	John Codman
Following the Frontier	Roger Pocock
On Horseback in Virginia	Charles Dudley Warner
California Coast Trails	J. Smeaton Chase
My Kingdom for a Horse	Margaret Leigh
The Journeys of Celia Fiennes	Celia Fiennes
On Horseback through Asia Minor	Fred Burnaby
The Abode of Snow	Andrew Wilson
A Lady's Life in the Rocky Mountains	Isabella Bird
Travels in Afghanistan	Ernest F. Fox
Through Mexico on Horseback	Joseph Carl Goodwin
Caucasian Journey	Negley Farson
Turkestan Solo	Ella K. Maillart
Through the Highlands of Shropshire	Magdalene M. Weale
Wartime Ride	J. W. Day
Across the Roof of the World	Wilfred Skrede
Woman on a Horse	Ana Beker
Saddles East	John W. Beard
Last of the Saddle Tramps	Messanie Wilkins
Ride a White Horse	William Holt
Manual of Pack Transportation	H. W. Daly
Horses, Saddles and Bridles	W. H. Carter
Notes on Elementary Equitation	Carleton S. Cooke
Cavalry Drill Regulations	United States Army
Horse Packing	Charles Johnson Post
14th Century Arabic Riding Manual	Muhammad al-Aqsarai
The Art of Travel	Francis Galton
Shanghai à Moscou	Madame de Bourboulon
Saddlebags for Suitcases	Mary Bosanquet
The Road to the Grey Pamir	Ana Louise Strong
Boot and Saddle in Africa	Thomas Lambie
To the Foot of the Rainbow	Clyde Kluckhohn
Through Five Republics on Horseback	George Ray
Journey from the Arctic	Donald Brown
Saddle and Canoe	Theodore Winthrop
The Prairie Traveler	Randolph Marcy
Reiter, Pferd und Fahrer – Volume One	Dr. C. Geuer
Reiter, Pferd und Fahrer – Volume Two	Dr. C. Geuer

The Long Riders' Guild
The world's leading source of information regarding equestrian exploration!
www.thelongridersguild.com